AQA Religiou Studies A

Philosophy of Religion

GCSE

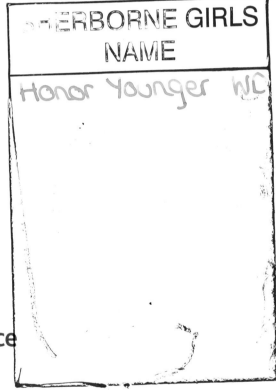

Peter Wallace

Series editor

Cynthia Bartlett

OXFORD
UNIVERSITY PRESS

OXFORD
UNIVERSITY PRESS

Great Clarendon Street, Oxford, OX2 6DP, United Kingdom

Oxford University Press is a department of the University of Oxford.
It furthers the University's objective of excellence in research, scholarship,
and education by publishing worldwide. Oxford is a registered trade mark of
Oxford University Press in the UK and in certain other countries

British Library Cataloguing in Publication Data
Data available

978-1-4085-0460-4

5

Printed in China

Acknowledgements

Cover photograph: Getty Images
Illustrations: Paul McCaffrey (C/ O Sylvie Poggio Agency)
Page make-up: Pantek Arts Ltd

The publisher would like to thank the following companies and individuals who assisted with this book: Indexing Specialists
(UK) Ltd.

The author and publisher are grateful to the following for permissions to the reproduce photographs and other copyright
material:

Text acknowledgements
Scripture quotations taken from the Holy Bible, New International Version. Copyright © 1978, 1984 by International Bible
Society. Used by permission of Hodder & Stoughton, a division of Hodder Headline Ltd. All rights reserved. 'NIV' is a registered
trademark of International Bible Society. UK trademark number 1448790; Auschwitz Memorial Museum and Jacek Lachendro
for an extract from the website en.auschwitz.org.pl for an extract on 'Living Conditions' by Jacek Lachendro; HarperCollins
Publishers for an extract from Icons Teacher's Resource Book 1 by M J Martin et al. Reprinted by permission of HarperCollins
Publishers Ltd, © M J Martin et al, 2001; fatima.org for an extract from 'Visions of the 'Three Seers''; Luxamore and Leonard
Glenroy Lie for an extract from the website www.indotalisman.com, The 99 Beautiful Divine Names of Allah; The Friends of
Julian Norwich for an extract from www.friendsofjulian.org.uk on the life and work of Julian of Norwich; The Holiday Spot for
an extract on Guru Nanak's enlightenment, from www.theholidayspot.com, a website that provides information about all the
popular festivals and holidays of the world.

Photo acknowledgements
Alamy; Corbis; Fotolia; Getty Images; iStockphoto. Special appreciation is offered to Frances Topp for photograph research.

Although we have made every effort to trace and contact all
copyright holders before publication this has not been possible in all
cases. If notified, the publisher will rectify any errors or omissions at
the earliest opportunity.

Links to third party websites are provided by Oxford in good faith
and for information only. Oxford disclaims any responsibility for
the materials contained in any third party website referenced in
this work.

Contents

The publisher has worked hard to make sure that this book offers you excellent support for your GCSE course.

☎ How to use this book

Learning Objectives

At the beginning of each section or topic you'll find a list of Learning Objectives based on the requirements of the specification, so you can make sure you cover the key points required.

Objectives

Objectives

Objectives

Objectives

First objective.

Second objective.

Study Tips

Don't forget to look at the Study Tips throughout the book to help you with your study and prepare for your exam.

Study tip

Don't forget to look at the Study Tips throughout the book to help you with your study and prepare for your exam.

Practice Questions

These offer opportunities to practise questions in the style that you may encounter in your exam so that you can be prepared on the day.

Practice questions are reproduced by permission of the Assessment and Qualifications Alliance.

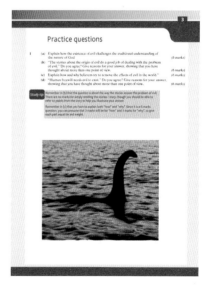

GCSE Philosophy of Religion

This book is written specifically for GCSE students studying the AQA Religious Studies Specification A, *Unit 7 Philosophy of Religion*. Religious philosophy is the study of how religions seek to give answers to the ultimate questions that face most people. Philosophy is the seeking of knowledge by asking questions and analysing the answers. Religion is the reaching beyond the present existence for ultimate answers.

This book and the GCSE course do not make any presumption about any student's beliefs. There are religious dimensions to all the topics studied and for the GCSE exam these dimensions have to be clearly examined. However, this particular course does not demand the study of a particular religion. Examples to support ideas can be taken from any number of religions or just one religion. The book is to help students think more deeply about these areas.

◼ Topics in this unit

In the examination you will be asked to answer five questions out of six that are based on the following six topics.

The existence of God

In this topic you will study the different arguments put forward to support the idea of a God that exists and to oppose this idea.

The characteristics of God

This topic examines how people can use limited words to discuss the unlimited God. It examines the meaningfulness and otherwise of common words used about God and asks whether it is helpful to use everyday words to help people latch onto central ideas about the nature of God.

Revelation and enlightenment

This topic examines how God can show himself to believers. It asks how valid these revelations are both for the recipient and for other people. It also examines whether the whole idea of God and religion are just human inventions.

The problem of evil

In this topic you will examine the perennial questions of how there can exist both a loving God and a lot of evil, and suffering in life. Common propositions like the free will defence and the need for the bad to enable us to value the good will be explored to find out if there are any acceptable solutions.

The compatibility of science and religion

This topic deals with the creation of the universe and the theory of evolution. It examines both the scientific and some religious arguments with the intention of establishing whether these two approaches are mutually exclusive.

The afterlife

You will examine different approaches to what happens after death, including contrasting the beliefs of those who believe in some form of resurrection with those who believe in some form of reincarnation. You will also question the validity of the evidence for any of these ideas.

◼ Assessment guidance

The exam paper is split into two parts. On Part A there are four questions worth in total 48 marks. The marks are equally divided between AO1 (facts and application) and AO2 (evaluation). On part B there are two questions each worth 24 marks, divided into four parts, again having the marks equally distributed between AO1 and AO2 questions. Candidates choose which of the two questions they will answer. AO1 questions can vary from 1 to 6 marks. AO2 questions will either be worth 3 marks (usually two questions a paper) or 6 marks.

Examination questions will test two assessment objectives:

AO1	Describe, explain and analyse, using knowledge and understanding.	50%
AO2	Use evidence and reasoned argument to express and evaluate personal responses, informed insights, and differing viewpoints.	50%

The quality of your written communication will also be taken into account – how clearly you express yourself and how well you communicate your meaning. The grid below also gives you some guidance on the sort of quality expected at different levels.

Levels of response mark scheme

Levels	Criteria for AO1	Criteria for AO2	Quality of written communication	Marks
0	Nothing relevant or worthy of credit	An unsupported opinion or no relevant evaluation	The candidate's presentation, spelling, punctuation and grammar seriously obstruct understanding	0 marks
Level 1	Something relevant or worthy of credit	An opinion supported by simple reason	The candidate presents some relevant information in a simple form. The text produced is usually legible. Spelling, punctuation and grammar allow meaning to be derived, although errors are sometimes obstructive	1 mark
Level 2	Elementary knowledge and understanding, e.g. two simple points	An opinion supported by one developed reason or two simple reasons		2 marks
Level 3	Sound knowledge and understanding	An opinion supported by one well developed reason or several simple reasons. N.B. Candidates who make no religious comment should not achieve more than Level 3	The candidate presents relevant information in a way which assists with the communication of meaning. The text produced is legible. Spelling, punctuation and grammar are sufficiently accurate not to obscure meaning	3 marks
Level 4	A clear knowledge and understanding with some development	An opinion supported by two developed reasons with reference to religion		4 marks
Level 5	A detailed answer with some analysis, as appropriate	Evidence of reasoned consideration of two different points of view, showing informed insights and knowledge and understanding of religion	The candidate presents relevant information coherently, employing structure and style to render meaning clear. The text produced is legible. Spelling, punctuation and grammar are sufficiently accurate to render meaning clear	5 marks
Level 6	A full and coherent answer showing good analysis, as appropriate	A well-argued response, with evidence of reasoned consideration of two different points of view showing informed insights and ability to apply knowledge and understanding of religion effectively		6 marks

Please note that mark schemes change over time. Please refer to the AQA website for the very latest information.

Note: In evaluation answers to questions worth only 3 marks, the first three levels apply. Questions which are marked out of 3 marks do not ask for two views, but reasons for your own opinion.

Successful study of this unit will result in a Short Course GCSE award. Study of one further unit will provide a Full Course GCSE award. Other units in Specification A which may be taken to achieve a Full Course GCSE award are:

- Unit 1 Christianity
- Unit 2 Christianity: Ethics
- Unit 3 Roman Catholicism
- Unit 4 Roman Catholicism: Ethics
- Unit 5 St Mark's Gospel
- Unit 6 St Luke's Gospel
- Unit 8 Islam
- Unit 9 Islam: Ethics
- Unit 10 Judaism
- Unit 11 Judaism: Ethics
- Unit 12 Buddhism
- Unit 13 Hinduism
- Unit 14 Sikhism

1 The existence of God

1.1 The existence of God

People's approaches

People have different attitudes towards the existence of God. The three most common attitudes are:

- **theism** – a person who believes there is a God is called a **theist**
- **atheism** – a person who says there is no such thing as God is called an **atheist**
- **agnosticism** – a person who does not know if there is a God or not and who is not convinced by the arguments either way is called an **agnostic**.

A *A theist believes in a God who cares*

Activities

1. Ask 20 people whether they would call themselves theist, atheist or agnostic. What is the balance of opinion in the group you ask?
2. Explain which of these words would apply to you.
3. Which of these views do you think is the easiest view to hold? Why?
4. What difference would holding each of these views make to the way people would lead their lives?

What is God?

It is very difficult to define God but most people would say that God is the supreme being who has no limits in time, space or power. For Jews, Christians and Muslims and other monotheists, God is seen as the Creator of the universe. Some of the terms used about God include omnipotent (all-powerful), omniscient (all-knowing) and benevolent (loving).

What is proof?

Proof is the evidence that establishes a fact or the truth of a statement. Genuine proof cannot be rejected by anybody who is open-minded and totally honest, as proof should remove all areas of doubt in a person's mind.

Proof is usually of a physical nature, for example seeing something with your own eyes, or the result of a well-conducted experiment. Sometimes, in a court of law, all the evidence put together can act as proof.

Can the existence of God be proved?

Many people have tried to prove the existence of God. However, there are some problems with this:

- As human beings, we can only prove things with our physical senses: smell, sight, touch, and so on.
- God cannot be proved by humans using their physical senses as this would mean that what is proved is physical. Anything proved using the physical senses cannot be God.
- Physical beings have limitations, which means they are not infinite.
- 'Evidence', such as people claiming to experience God through a vision or through hearing God, is not really valid for other people. It is only valid for the person who has had the experience.
- Some people argue that only logic and reason can show that God must exist. The question is: how valid are logic and reason as proof?

links

For definitions of these words (omnipotent, omniscient, benevolent), see the Glossary on pages 140–141.

B   *God is all-knowing, all-powerful and loving*

Research activity

Think about the different types of proof that people are normally willing to accept, for example: scientific evidence, the evidence of their own eyes, the evidence offered to a jury in a court of law, physical evidence. Which of these types of proof do you find most useful or believable and why?

Extension activity

Many countries have an official position towards religion(s). This gives some idea of the attitude towards God that the country's leaders prefer. Choose three countries and find out what their official religious policy is.

Discussion activities

1   Who won last year's Cup Final? How do you know? What would you say to anybody who challenged your answer?

2   Do you love your parents? Where is the proof? Do your parents love you? Where is the proof?

3   Some people say you cannot prove God. Are they just trying to get out of an argument? Explain your opinion.

4   Faith can be seen as a leap into the unknown. Why do many people say they have faith in God? Could you have faith in God if you could prove God exists? Explain your opinion.

Summary

You should now know that there are many different attitudes to the existence of God. God cannot be proved by any scientific method. Some people say that God cannot exist because He cannot be proved.

The first cause argument for the existence of God

When dealing with the existence of God, physical evidence is not available to prove that God does exist. Many thinkers use the term 'argument' as a word that means a presentation of an idea. Although 'argument' usually means people having a heated debate, in this context argument means a set of reasons to support an idea.

■ The First Cause Argument

The **first cause argument** is sometimes called the **cosmological** argument, as it is to do with the nature of the cosmos or universe. Many thinkers have supported this approach, most notably St Thomas Aquinas (1226–1274 CE). He drew up five ways to prove the existence of God. The first three of these ways are all cosmological arguments.

The first way:

- We see things moving.
- Things do not move themselves, but have to be moved by something else.
- However, that 'something else' had to be moved by something that existed before it. This cannot go back to infinity as there would be no starting movement and, therefore, no second movement.
- Things must have been moved by something that, in itself, was not moved by anything else. This is called 'God'.

The first way depends on the idea of motion, that is, any change from one natural state to another. An example of this is a person's hair going grey because of a change in their metabolism. All changes or movements happen as a result of something else; they do not just happen on their own. There has to be a starting point to this whole process, but this starting point could not have been moved or brought into being by anything else. It must just be.

The second way:

- Everything has a cause.
- Nothing makes itself happen, but everything depends on another thing to make it happen.
- This cannot go back to infinity as there would be no first cause and so no subsequent cause.
- There must have been an uncaused cause. This is called 'God'.

This second way is very straightforward and follows the pattern of the first way. In life, everything we experience is caused by something else. For example, a door does not open on its own; it has to be pushed open by a person, a dog, the wind or something else. Everything follows this pattern. However, there has to have been a first thing that made everything else respond or react. If there were no first cause, then there is nothing that happens in life. Simply looking around you shows that things happen in life.

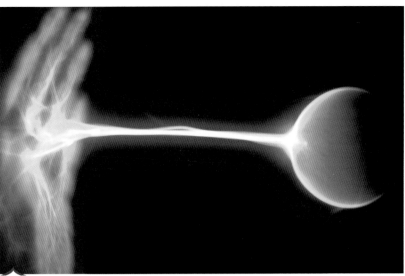

A   *Something has to be there to cause something else*

Research activity

Find out all you can about Thomas Aquinas (1225–1274).

Extension activity

1   Use the internet and/or a library to research either:

a   the Kalam cosmological argument

b   what Leibnitz (1646–1716) says in his Principle of Sufficient Reason.

The third way:

- Everything comes into being and goes out of being, meaning they either exist or do not exist.
- But this means that there must have been a time when there was nothing.
- If there was nothing, then something cannot come from nothing.
- Therefore, something must always have existed. This is called 'God'.

The third way depends on the fact that everything we experience in this life has to exist. Everything is dependent on something else. However, if this were true about absolutely everything, then there would be nothing now. The fact that I am here writing this book, and you are reading it, proves that something exists. There has to be something that exists. It cannot not exist or else there would be nothing now.

Case study

Philip is a 35 year old scientist who says: 'I think Thomas Aquinas has a lot of clear points in what he says. There must have always been something otherwise there would be nothing here now. Even if scientists prove that the Universe has always existed, they will need to explain how it got here. Something cannot come from nothing.'

What do you think about Philip's point of view? Explain your answer.

Discussion activities

1   As a group choose one of these three ways and put it in your own words to present to the rest of the class.

2   Do any of these ways make sense to you? Explain your answer.

3   What have your teacher, an elephant, a chair, Mount Everest and the planet Neptune got in common? Does this suggest anything to you about the above arguments?

4   As a group, can you think of any weaknesses in the arguments put forward so far? Explain your thoughts.

Summary

You should now understand the first cause argument which says that because there is something that exists now, this can only be explained by the fact that there has always been something. Movement and cause cannot go back to infinity. They must have had a starting point, and this starting point is God, who is unmoved and uncaused.

Arguments about the first cause argument for the existence of God

Why is there something rather than nothing?

Another form of the first cause argument asks the very simple question: why is there anything at all? Could things just have happened?

Looking at the universe, scientists would claim that the universe we know probably started with a big bang. About 15 billion years ago, there was a mighty explosion of an infinitely dense point (called a singularity) and from this explosion came all the material that forms the universe. People have various opinions on this theory:

- For some people this is enough to explain the universe. For example, Bertrand Russell (1872–1970) said, 'I should say the universe is just there, and that's all'. However, many people cannot accept this statement as it does not answer the question about **why** the universe or anything exists. This important question appears to be dismissed as unimportant.

- People ask where the big bang came from, and take the question further back from there. Many come back to the argument that there must be a starting point.

- There must be pure being (or pure existence) for there to be anything at all, including the materials that created the big bang. God is pure being or pure existence. God is infinite. If God is infinite being (existence) then anything else that is infinite (such as love, knowledge or power) must all be in God as there cannot be more than one infinite.

Objectives

Examine what arguments might be used to reinforce the first cause argument.

Examine what arguments are used to show that the first cause argument does not prove its case.

Evaluate both sides of this argument.

∞ links

See pages 110–111 for more details on the big bang.

A *Is this how creation started? If so how does God fit in?*

Activities

1 Was Russell right to say, 'the universe is just there, and that's all'? Explain your answer.

2 Try to think of something that does not need an explanation.

Arguments against the first cause

David Hume (1711–1776) argued:

- Just because we normally think of things having a cause or being moved, this does not mean that this has to apply to the whole universe.
- Our experience of things is limited to what happens within our world. Things outside our world and universe could work totally differently.
- We cannot jump to the conclusion that things need to be explained in the way Aquinas tried to do.
- Maybe things have always existed back to infinity.
- Some people claim that the universe cannot just be explained by itself, but can only be explained by the existence of God. However, they are happy to say that God can just be explained by himself. Why are they happy to accept an unexplained God, but not an unexplained universe?
- If God is perfect, why is the universe he made full of imperfections? Does this not suggest that the God who made it is imperfect (and so not God)?
- Couldn't this universe have been the efforts of a young God trying his hand at things but getting it wrong?
- Just because the universe might need a cause, does this mean that the cause is infinite?

Activity

3   'The first cause argument does not prove that there is a God who cares.' Do you agree? Give reasons for your answer showing that you have thought about more than one point of view.

Activities

4   Look at Hume's arguments and say what you think are the strongest points and the weakest points in what he says.

5   'The first cause argument does not prove that God exists.' Do you agree? Give reasons for your answer, showing that you have thought about more than one point of view.

Does the first cause argument lead to a belief in one God?

Some people are happy to accept the idea that the first cause argument leads to the idea of a first cause, but they stop at that point. They do not think that a person can say any more about that first cause. They think it is wrong to make the leap from a first cause to say anything about that cause being the caring, personal God that is essential to Judaism, Christianity and Islam. They cannot accept the idea that the first cause has to be infinite in every dimension.

Extension activity

Use the internet and/or a library to find out as much as you can about what either Jews or Christians or Muslims say about the nature of their God. Compare this to a God that might be proved if the first cause argument is convincing. What do your findings suggest to you about the validity of the first cause argument?

Summary

You should now know that people argue for and against the first cause argument. Even if a first cause makes sense, some people believe that this does not mean there has to be a God.

The design argument for the existence of God

The design argument

The **design argument** for the existence of God is sometimes called the **teleological argument**, from the Greek word 'telos' which means design or purpose. It is based on the understanding that there is a design in creation and if there is a design there must be a designer and this designer is God.

Paley's watch

William Paley (1743–1805 CE) came up with one of the most famous examples of the design argument. He said that if, on a walk, you stumbled over a stone, you would not question its existence; you would be happy just to accept the fact that it is there. However, if a few minutes later you find an old-fashioned watch, with its complex mechanism, you would not simply accept that it just happened. You would insist that there had to be a maker of that watch. Paley argued that the same applied to the whole of creation. There is so much order in creation that it could not just have happened. It must have been created by an intelligent designer (God).

Objectives

Examine the design argument for the existence of God.

Evaluate the design argument.

Key terms

Argument from design: a proof for the existence of God based on the idea that there is so much design and purpose in the universe that it could not have happened by accident; there has to have been a designer–God. Otherwise called the teleological argument.

Teleological: to do with design or order, particularly the attempt to prove the existence of God by showing that there is design and order in the universe.

A *Does the existence of these rocks need to be explained?*

B *Does the existence of this clockwork watch need explaining?*

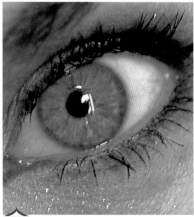

C *Does the existence of a perfectly functioning eye need explaining?*

Activities

1. What is the difference between a rock, a watch and an eye?
2. Do you think the existence of any of these can lead to proving the existence of God? Explain your answer.

Aquinas' design argument

Aquinas had a similar theory, but he used a different illustration.

  Aquinas used the idea of an arrow and an archer to support his design argument

Aquinas argued that an arrow will not hit a target just by itself. It needs someone to intend to shoot it towards, the target. Furthermore, the shape of the arrow, the weighting and balance, the design of the feathers and so forth all play their part to help the arrow to hit the bullseye. None of this could just happen. In the same way, the whole of creation needs an intelligent designer for there to be order and purpose within it.

Study tip

Learn the different examples used by William Paley and Thomas Aquinas to help explain the design argument – they will help you to remember the main points of the argument.

Research activity

Choose any object and show how it has been designed or made for a particular function. Would it be possible to say that this item just came into being on its own? Explain your answer.

Discussion activities

1. What are the strong points and the weak points in Aquinas' design argument?

2. Which example (the arrow or the watch) do you think best supports the design argument? Explain your answer.

3. How far do you agree with Vera's opinion? Explain your answer.

Case study

Vera is a 70 year old who spends a lot of time knitting pullovers. She says: 'When I sit down to start a new pullover, I have to have a good idea of exactly what I am going to end up with. I cannot simply let the needles move on their own otherwise the end result will be a total mess. I think the same thing applies to the world and the Universe. If God did not design it, things would be totally out of control. The fact that there is order and not chaos proves to me that there is a God behind creation.'

Summary

You should now understand that some people say that there is so much order and design in the world that a perfect being must have created it.

Arguments about the design argument for the existence of God

Is there order in creation?

There are many views on whether there is order in creation. For example:

- Some people claim that creation is a very ordered thing with every part depending on the others to produce a complex whole. An example of this is the way animals cooperate to produce a balance in nature, which is important for the survival of the whole species.
- There is just the right balance of chemicals in the air and earth to allow for the evolution and development of human beings, which suggests there is a design.
- Other people argue that the only order we see is the order we impose on things to make them manageable.
- Some people think that everything is just random and haphazard. They believe that it is simply pure luck that we happen to live at a time of relative order, but this might soon end.
- Some people think that human beings do not like to feel that they are in a place of chaos so have created an illusion of order to make them feel better.

Does the amount of evil and disorder in the world argue against a perfect God?

Some people think that the number of things that go wrong in the world raises questions about the nature and ability of any creator.

- If God made the world, some people claim that he can only be an incompetent or limited being and not an all-powerful God.
- However, if the world is simply a result of chance, then disasters do not need explaining.

Evolution and chance

Charles Darwin (1802–1882 CE) developed the theory of evolution. This idea is based on the idea of the survival of the fittest, meaning that if something is best adapted to a situation it will thrive whereas something that is not adapted to the situation will not be able to survive and reproduce. This is called natural selection.

Some people would argue that this approach covers the whole of creation: things will only develop if the situation is right. An example of this is that the earth happened to be in the right position relative to the sun for water and oxygen to develop which allowed life to prosper and humanity to grow. In other words it was the result of a lucky set of chances, not the end product of a specific, designed intention.

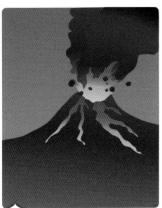

A   *Do these disasters raise questions about order in the world?*

Does the design argument prove the existence of God?

There are many views on whether the design argument proves the existence of God:

- Some people think that the design argument is the strongest of the arguments. They would say that because there is so much order in the universe, it could not happen without a guiding mind or God.

- Others say that if there was a God he would have made a better job of creating things.

- Since there are valid points on both sides of the argument, some people feel that their only honest response is to say that the design argument does not actually prove that God exists, though parts of it might suggest that the existence of God is probable.

Summary

You should now understand that people have different views on whether there is order in creation. Some think the design argument is the best way to prove that God exists but other people question whether the design argument works at all.

Research activity

Use the internet and/or a library to examine one event that would be classed as a natural disaster. What evidence might lead you to say that there are both good and bad aspects to this disaster?

Extension activity

Research the views of John Stuart Mill (1806–1873) against the Design Argument. How valid do you think his arguments are?

Activity

3   'The design argument does not prove the existence of God.' Do you agree? Give reasons for your answer, showing that you have thought about more than one point of view.

The argument for the existence of God from religious experience

What is experience?

People experience things all the time. Experience is an integral part of living. Most of the time we use our senses to help us respond to the situations around us that create our experiences.

Some people deliberately put themselves into situations that heighten their experiences, for example bungee jumping or doing extreme physical exercise.

Often it is impossible to put our experience into words, as words cannot communicate what we are trying to express. Experiences make us aware of being alive, but they also teach us new things about ourselves and other people.

Objectives

Examine what is meant by an experience.

Examine how religious experience is different to other experiences.

Evaluate how valid religious experiences are.

A *What are people trying to experience when they do extreme sports?*

B *How does this mother feel at this moment? Is this like a religious experience?*

Activities

1. Try to put into words how you felt when the dentist last drilled one of your teeth or pulled a tooth out. Why is this not easy to do?

2. Try to tell someone who has never had either strawberries or ice cream what strawberry ice cream tastes like. How easy is this? Why?

3. Imagine what it would feel like to be born (as some people are) without any sensation. What difficulties would there be for people in this situation?

■ What is religious experience?

Religion is defined in the *Concise Oxford Dictionary* as 'the belief in and worship of a super-human controlling power, especially a personal God or gods; a particular system of faith and worship'.

Faith is a leap into the unknown, into something that cannot be proved as it goes beyond the things that are provable.

What does this mean for those who have experiences and those who hear about them?

There are several issues around religious experiences:

- People have an awareness of having a contact with an outside supreme being that they cannot deny to themselves. Their feelings about this experience and their awareness of it are too strong to be denied.
- Because religion is dealing with an absolute unlimited being, it is difficult to talk about or to explain to other people. The main reason for this is that words cannot convey what the person wants to say about God.
- As with a toothache or the feeling gained from bungee jumping, the person who has a religious experience is fully involved in the sensation. However, outsiders can only accept the description of the experience that they are given.
- Even if outsiders have had personal religious experiences similar to that described to them, because everybody is unique and individual, religious experiences are also unique and individual.
- However, because religious experiences can make a great difference to the people who have had them, other people might accept what they are told about the experience and use this information as a basis for their own acceptance of the faith. A classic case of this is the number of people who have accepted the resurrection of Jesus as a fact based on the experience of the early disciples and their claims to have seen the Risen Christ.

Research activity

Interview four people about their experiences, perhaps when they have been in love or have attended a very moving concert or event of some type. Compare these accounts to accounts of religious experiences. It would be good if the same person could talk about both religious and non-religious experiences so you can compare the type of language and feelings expressed.

∞links

To explore more about the difficulty of using words to talk about God, see pages 39–53.

Activities

4   Why is it difficult to talk about religious experiences?

5   'Outsiders have to accept that what people tell them about their own religious experiences is based on fact.' Do you agree? Give reasons for your answer, showing that you have thought about more than one point of view.

Study tip

Remember that for 6-mark questions you have to present at least two sides of an argument, even if you do not accept one or any of the points you present. Marks come for how well you deal with the arguments, not for what you believe.

Summary

You should now understand that life is based on people having experiences that help them to develop. Religious experiences come from outside the physical world and are difficult to put into words. Other people might accept what they are told about religious experiences.

Accounts of religious experiences (1)

■ Cases of religious experiences

Many people say that they have had a religious experience. The most common features of these events are that the experience was totally unexpected, totally overwhelming and life-changing.

The following are fairly typical examples chosen from those people who have given an account of their experience.

Objectives

Examine some cases studies of religious experiences.

Understand the differences these experiences made in the lives of believers.

Evaluate to what extent these experiences can be used to prove the existence of God.

Case study

The Call of Jeremiah

⁴The word of the Lord came to me, saying, ⁵'Before I formed you in the womb I knew you, before you were born I set you apart; I appointed you as a prophet to the nations.' ⁶'Ah, Sovereign Lord,' I said, 'I do not know how to speak; I am only a child.' ⁷But the Lord said to me, 'Do not say, "I am only a child." You must go to everyone I send you to and say whatever I command you. ⁸Do not be afraid of them, for I am with you and will rescue you,' declared the Lord. ⁹Then the Lord reached out his hand and touched my mouth and said to me, 'Now, I have put my words in your mouth. ¹⁰See, today I appoint you over nations and kingdoms to uproot and tear down, to destroy and overthrow, to build and to plant.'

Jeremiah 1:4–10

Case study

The Transfiguration

²After six days Jesus took Peter, James and John with him and led them up a high mountain, where they were all alone. There he was transfigured before them. ³His clothes became dazzling white, whiter than anyone in the world could bleach them. ⁴And there appeared before them Elijah and Moses, who were talking with Jesus. ⁵Peter said to Jesus, 'Rabbi, it is good for us to be here. Let us put up three shelters – one for you, one for Moses and one for Elijah.' ⁶(He did not know what to say, they were so frightened.) ⁷Then a cloud appeared and enveloped them, and a voice came from the cloud: 'This is my Son, whom I love. Listen to him!' ⁸Suddenly, when they looked around, they no longer saw anyone with them except Jesus.

Mark 9:2–8

A *The Transfiguration*

Research activity

1 Use the internet and/or a library to find out all you can about the prophet Jeremiah at the time of his call. What differences did this experience make to his life?

Case study

Julian of Norwich – her life and work

On 8 May 1373, when she was 30 years old, Julian suffered a severe illness from which she almost died. During that illness she received a series of visions of the Passion of Christ and the love of God. Following this experience, she became an anchoress at St Julian's and spent the remainder of her life in prayer and meditation, and offering comfort and advice to those who came to her window.

Over the course of some 20 years, Julian reflected on the meaning of her visions and wrote down an account of this.

From the time of her visions in 1373 until she finished her book some 20 years later, Julian puzzled over the question, 'What was our Lord's meaning?' At the end of this long journey, she received the answer:

'What, do you wish to know your Lord's meaning in this thing? Know it well, love was his meaning. Who reveals it to you? Love. What did he reveal to you? Love. Why does he reveal it to you? For love. … So I was taught that love is our Lord's meaning. And I saw very certainly in this and in everything that before God made us he loved us, which love was never abated and never will be.'

Source: www.friendsofjulian.org.uk

B *Julian of Norwich*

Research activity

2 Use the internet and/or a library to find out all you can about Julian of Norwich at the time of her visions. What differences did these visions make to her life?

3 Look up three other religious experiences contained in the Bible. Explain them in your own words.

Activities

1 Is it easy to make sense of these passages on pages 20 and 21? Explain your answer.

2 What reasons might be given for saying that these experiences actually happened?

Extension activity

There were many people in England in the 14th century who claimed to have visions, notably Marjory Kempe whose experiences are questioned by many Christians. Examine what the differences are between those whose visions are respected and those whose visions are suspected.

Summary

You should now understand that people who give accounts of a great religious experience are convinced that it has happened. Their lives are changed forever, even though other people may not accept what they have to say about their experiences.

Case study

The First Revelation to Muhammad

Tradition has it that Muhammad often used to meditate in a cave near Makkah, where he could find the peace and quiet he needed. The cave was in a mountain called the Mountain of Light and the cave has come to be known as Hira. When Muhammad was forty years old, he received his first revelation. It happened during the month of Ramadan, or the month of heat.

Muhammad heard a voice telling him to read. Since he didn't have any text, Muhammad answered 'I cannot read.' The voice told him a second and then a third time, 'Read!', and Muhammad finally answered, 'What can I read?'

The voice said:

'Read: In the name of thy Lord Who createth

Createth man from a clot.

Read: And it is thy Lord the Most Bountiful

Who teacheth by the pen,

Teacheth man that which he knew not.'

After hearing this Muhammad went out of the cave. On the mountainside he was told by the same voice that he had been chosen as Allah's messenger and that the voice he was hearing was an angel, Gabriel. Muhammad looked up and saw Gabriel, surrounded by light, hovering in the sky. The vision was so bright that Muhammad turned his face away to shield his eyes, but wherever he turned, the angel was right in front of him. The vision continued for a long time until the angel eventually vanished. Later, a wise and very old man called Waraqa ibn Nawfal declared to the people that Muhammad had seen the same messenger that had appeared to Moses anciently, and that Muhammad had been chosen to be a Prophet.

Objectives

Examine some cases studies of religious experiences.

Understand the differences these experiences made in the lives of believers.

Evaluate to what extent these experiences can be used to prove the existence of God.

Research activity

Research accounts of religious experiences from two different religions. Examine what these accounts have in common (if anything) and where the major differences (if any) occur between them.

A *The cave where Muhammad received the Qur'an at Hira*

John Wesley

John Wesley (1703–1791 CE), who founded the Methodist Church, was an Anglican clergyman when he had the following experience:

In the evening I went very unwillingly to a society in Aldersgate Street, where one was reading Luther's preface to the Epistle to the Romans. About a quarter before nine, while he was describing the change which God works in the heart through faith in Christ, I felt my heart strangely warmed. I felt I did trust in Christ, Christ alone, for salvation; and an assurance was given me, that he had taken away my sins, even mine, and saved me from the law of sin and death.

Quoted from W. Raeper, Beginner's Guide to Ideas

   John Wesley, founder of the Methodist Church

Activities

1   Choose one of these passages and explain why the person might have had the experience.

2   If the experience did not come from God, what other explanation could you offer? Is this alternative convincing in the light of the person's subsequent life story? Explain your answer.

Father Francis is a 60 year old priest who has served in parishes in different parts of the country during his 35 years as a priest. He says: 'I think there are so many things that can class as a religious experience that it would be easy to overlook a lot of them. We have long accounts of major visions or unusual events that change people's lives in dramatic ways. But I think that most religious experiences are very quiet, unsung events that gently nudge people along the path that is right for them. Meeting the love of your life on a blind date or suddenly realising that the most important thing for you to do is to become a nurse and care for the elderly can be as much a religious experience as hearing voices from heaven. If people are open to the presence of God in their lives, they can feel him near and guiding them. You cannot prove that there is a God in this way, but for those who are uncertain or who already believe in God, these events can develop or reinforce their beliefs.'

Extension activity

Interview two people from different backgrounds (or if possible, from two different religious traditions) who claim they have had religious experiences of some type. Make a detailed account of their experiences.

Discussion activity

As a class, compile a collection of religious experiences. Try to explain why you would treat some of these accounts with more respect than others. Compare your findings with each other and see if you can come to some overall agreement about which religious experiences were the most meaningful.

Summary

You should now understand that people who give accounts of a great religious experience are convinced that it has happened. Their lives are changed forever, even though many other people may not accept what they have to say about their experiences.

1.9 How valid is the argument from religious experience for the existence of God?

▌ Points in favour of the argument from religious experience

Objectives

Examine arguments for and against the idea that religious experience proves the existence of God.

Evaluate these arguments.

A	People who actually have religious experiences cannot deny what has happened to them, even though they might have difficulty in putting the experience into words.
B	Most valid religious experiences come unexpectedly. The person who has the experience has not done anything to prepare for it, so cannot be accused of 'making it happen' by wish-fulfilment, mental aberration or anything similar.
C	Most people whose religious experiences are respected by believers are down-to-earth people who are usually quite shy of giving an account of what has happened to them.
D	Religious experiences happen to people of all religions, social classes and educational backgrounds. It cannot be claimed that they only happen to people who are unrefined or non-scientific.
E	People who write or talk about their religious experiences often give a very authentic account that stands up to careful examination.
F	The fact that so many people have similar types of experiences that they link to their God strongly suggests that there must be a God to give these experiences. If there were no God, these experiences would not happen or would be shown to be pointless.
G	Some religious experiences (such as the stigmata, which are marks on the hands similar to the scars that Jesus had following his crucifixion and resurrection) leave physical signs that often inconvenience or embarrass the person who has them.

A Points in favour of the argument from religious experience

Activity

1 Go through the list of points in favour of religious experiences proving the existence of God in Table A and say which you think make the strongest case.

B What does this statue suggest about religious experiences?

Study tip

Do not let your own religious belief or lack of belief influence your judgement. Try to look impartially at the evidence and present the case from both sides.

Points against the argument from religious experience

H	There is no evidence that the people who claim to have had religious experiences are actually telling the truth.
I	It is strange that nobody has a religious experience that would help them believe in a religion that they know nothing about. Some people might be converted by a religious experience relating to a religion that they have been studying for any number of reasons, often to find information that will show that that particular religion is wrong, for example Saul, a good Jew, having an experience of Jesus on the road to Damascus. No Christian has reported having an experience of a Hindu god. The people who report having visions of Mary are already Roman Catholics etc. Does this suggest that people's minds are trained in a very limited way and that they interpret everything in the way they have been trained?
J	Factors such as certain foods, alcohol or drugs make people have strange feelings. Could it be that these so-called religious experiences are simply people misunderstanding what is happening to them?
K	There are times when there seems to be an increase in reported religious experiences. Does this show that people jump on a 'bandwagon' of what is expected? Or does it show that people will only report their experiences when the climate for accepting that religious experiences happen is right?
L	If God gives religious experiences that people cannot deny, why doesn't he give them to everybody so that there is no doubt anywhere that God exists?
M	People who have religious experiences have often had some form of religious upbringing. This means that when they have the mysterious experience the obvious explanation for them is that it was a religious experience.

C Points against the argument from religious experience

D A religious experience?

Summary

You should now understand that people's lives can be transformed by religious experiences, which might prove that something special has happened. For many people who have a religious experience, this is enough proof that God exists. However, some people question where these experiences come from.

1.10 Faith

What is faith?

Here are some important points to remember about **faith**:

- Faith is a commitment to something that cannot be totally proved, but that is not contrary to facts.
- Faith is a different type of thing to knowledge. Faith is a leap into the unknown and unknowable. Knowledge is based on facts, or what can be proved.
- If a thing that was believed in were shown to be a fact, then it would no longer be a matter of faith. For example, if the Loch Ness Monster appeared and people were able to do scientific tests to prove it actually existed, nobody could say, 'I believe in Nessie'; they could only say, 'I know Nessie exists'.

Activity

1. There is a major difference between: 'I know it rained this morning' and 'I think it will rain tomorrow'.

   a. Explain the difference between these two statements.

   b. Write three other statements that show the difference between knowledge and belief.

Examples of faith

Case study

The Call of Abram

[1]The Lord had said to Abram, 'Leave your country, your people and your father's household and go to the land I will show you. [2] I will make you into a great nation and I will bless you; I will make your name great, and you will be a blessing. [3] I will bless those who bless you, and whoever curses you I will curse; and all peoples on earth will be blessed through you.' [4] So Abram left, as the Lord had told him; and Lot went with him. Abram was seventy-five years old when he set out from Haran.

Genesis 12:1–4

The call of Abram (whose name was later changed to Abraham) is a typical example of a man's response to faith. Abram was a wealthy, childless old man and he was called by God to commit himself to God alone. He had to leave all his security and protection and go to an unknown land among foreign people. God promised him that he would be the father of a great nation, a promise that seemed absurd from any human reasoning. This is a clear case of a person whose faith leads him to trust in God, despite all the known facts.

Objectives

Know the difference between faith and knowledge.

Understand how faith leads a person to make a positive commitment through actions.

Be aware of the limits of faith.

Key terms

Faith: a commitment to something that goes beyond proof and knowledge, especially used about God and religion.

Research activity

Research accounts of people who have made a commitment to their faith. What differences did this commitment make to their lives? Do you think they made wise decisions? Explain your answer.

Activities

2. Discuss whether Abram was sensible to do what God asked.

3. 'Faith can make people do stupid things.' Do you agree? Give reasons for your answer, showing that you have thought about more than one point of view.

A made-up story

The flood waters were rising fast. The passengers in a boat saw a man clinging to a roof. 'Room for one more,' they shouted. 'Come on!'

'No thanks,' shouted the man, 'I trust in God to save me.'

The waters rose higher and a lifeboat came along. The lifeboat men called to the man to come down. He refused their help with the same answer. By now the water was lapping around his feet, but he said the same to a rescue helicopter and its crew.

They flew away. The waters rose and the man drowned.

When he got to heaven he complained to God. 'I trusted in you and you didn't help me.'

'Well,' said God, 'I did send two boats and a helicopter.'

This story is taken from 'Pause for Thought', from Icons 2, Collins *Educational (2001), p52*

A

Activities

4 Was the man in the story right to do what he did? Explain your answer.

5 What does this story suggest about the nature of faith and actions?

A true story

During the Second World War in Auschwitz concentration camp, one day the Jewish prisoners realised that there were enough rabbis among them to set up a formal Jewish court. They put God on trial and said that if God existed and loved the Jewish people he would not let them suffer in the way they were suffering. They organised the formal court, heard all the evidence and finally found God guilty, accepting that he did not exist. At the end of the trial, the leading judge said to all the Jews there: 'Brethren, it is the time for evening prayer to God. Let us pray.'

B *The gates at Auschwitz*

Activities

6 Why did the Jews accept that God did not exist?

7 Why did they then complete the evening prayer?

8 What does this incident show about the relationship between proof and faith?

Study tip

Work out the difference between faith and knowledge before you try to show how each of them are shown in these events.

Summary

You should now know that faith is a commitment to something that cannot be totally proved, but which is not against reason.

1.11 Arguments against the existence of God and the nature of faith

Arguments against the existence of God

Many people believe that the evidence used in the attempted proof for the existence of God actually disproves that God exists. These points need to be looked at in the context of the proofs presented earlier.

Objectives

Examine why some people feel that there is enough evidence to reject the existence of God.

Evaluate the strength of these counter-arguments.

Examine whether it is possible to believe in God if there were proof that he really existed.

A	Why do we need to invent a God to make sense of what we do not know at the moment? Surely our knowledge of the universe is increasing daily and eventually we will come to understand how things began and we will be able to get rid of the idea of God once and for all.
B	Evolution has shown that there is not a specific design in the universe, just the way things have managed to adapt and survive to suit the situation. If the earth were different, the type of creatures that might inhabit the world would be different. Again, we do not need a God to explain things. This is just the way things are!
C	There is so much needless pain and suffering in this world. If there were an all-loving, all-powerful God, he would have done a better job at making the world and letting people be happy. Therefore, God cannot exist.
D	If God exists why does he not let us know about himself? Why do so many people believe in different gods and follow different, often contradictory, rules? If there was a perfect God surely everybody should be able to know Him and follow just one set of truths, not a vast array of them?

A *Arguments against the existence of God*

Activities

1. Choose one of the statements in Table **A** and prepare to either defend it or attack it in a debate.
2. Which do you think is the strongest of the arguments against the existence of God? Explain your answer.
3. Draw up a chart comparing the arguments for and against the existence of God.

Case study

Jenny is a 22 year old student who has been trying to examine the question of God's existence. She says: 'I do not think anybody will be able to prove that God exists because for every point in favour of God's existence, there is a valid argument against God's existence. I don't like being an agnostic, but I have not yet been persuaded by any of the arguments. Maybe in the end I will have to accept the fact that dealing with God is to go beyond human reason.'

What do you think about Jenny's comments?

B *Is there a God?*

Faith and God

Some people would argue that humans cannot know God. This is not so much because humans are not able to understand God's infinite power, but, rather, because if humans knew God existed they would have no option but to do what he said. They would have to obey him, worship him, etc., as they would not want to throw away eternal happiness, if that is what he offered.

For humans to be free, they must be able to question whether God exists or not and to freely reject him or accept him. Being free means being able to accept the consequences of our decisions. God would not want people to simply do as he said, like puppets.

If God could be proved definitively, human freedom would cease to exist.

Therefore, it is essential for human beings that they cannot definitely prove that God exists.

Activity

4 'The best thing that God can do for human beings is to let them doubt his existence.' Do you agree? Give reasons for your answer, showing that you have thought about more than one point of view.

Case study

Susan is a 50 year old housewife. She says: 'I believe in God. I know I cannot prove that God exists, but quite honestly I don't think it would help me even if I could prove beyond doubt that God exists. I am not trying to sound holy or anything like that, but if I only did things out of fear of God, I would not have any respect for God. As it is, I am happy to let God guide my life, trusting that he will see me through all the ups and downs. I am not really interested in these proofs for God's existence. I don't think they will ever come to anything anyway.'

Discussion activities

1   What do you think about Susan's comments?

2   With a partner, discuss the two case studies. Take one of the case studies each and rehearse the arguments Jenny and Susan are making. Which set of arguments do you find the most convincing?

Summary

You should now understand that many of the arguments for the existence of God can be turned around to prove that God does not exist. If people could prove definitively that God did exist, that would remove the possibility of faith and freedom for human beings.

links

For more details on free will see pages 94–95.

Study tip

Try to use a parallel case to understand the need for faith, not proof, for the existence of God. For example, if you had a 100 per cent guarantee that you would win the jackpot on the National Lottery if you did not eat for two days and put the money you saved into buying tickets, would you do it? Would you really be taking a gamble here? What would this mean for anybody else who wanted a gamble?

1

The existence of God – summary

For the examination, you should now be able to:

✔ explain why it is difficult to prove that God exists, and what is the nature of faith

✔ explain the strengths and weaknesses of the First Cause argument

✔ explain the strengths and weaknesses of the Design (Teleological) argument

✔ explain the argument from religious experience for the existence of God, its strengths and weaknesses

✔ explain the arguments against the existence of God

✔ evaluate the proofs in the light of the nature of God and faith.

Sample answer

1 Write an answer to the following exam question:

Explain the first cause argument for the existence of God.

(4 marks)

2 Read the following sample answer.

> The first cause argument is based on the idea that things do not just happen. Something cannot come from nothing. For anything to exist, there has to be existence. If there is no God, then there is nothing. So there has to be an uncaused cause, which is God.

3 With a partner, discuss the sample answer. Do you think there are other things the student could have included in the answer?

4 What mark would you give this answer out of 4? Look at the mark scheme in the Introduction on page 7 (AO1). What are the reasons for the mark you have given?

Practice questions

1 Look at the picture below and answer the following questions.

(a) Explain how religious experiences might be used to prove that God exists. *(6 marks)*

(b) 'All religious experiences are just made up and cannot be used to prove anything.' Do you agree? Give reasons for your answer, showing that you have thought about more than one point of view. *(6 marks)*

(c) Explain what is meant by the design argument. *(6 marks)*

(d) 'It is easier to believe in God than not to believe in God.' Do you agree? Give reasons for your answer, showing that you have thought about more than one point of view. *(6 marks)*

Study tip Note that in part (a) you are asked to deal with religious experience, and in part (c) about the design argument. It is important not to confuse the different arguments. Just because you studied them in one particular order does not mean that the exam paper will follow the same order.

2 The characteristics of God

2.1 God and images

God and words

Many human beings have an awareness of the presence of an ultimate force or being that is often referred to as God. However, because God is infinite, meaning he has no limits, it is difficult to use any words about Him in a way that actually makes sense.

To put this another way:

> Words are created by human beings. Humans are limited because they have a beginning and end, both in time and in space.

> Human minds have a very small capacity, possibly larger than any other creature, but still not able to cope with many things, certainly not many things at once.

> Because humans are limited, we cannot make sense of something that is infinite, such as God.

> All our efforts to understand or make sense of God are bound to fail.

> However, because humans feel the need to talk about this infinite being, to express and share what we do understand about him, we have to use the only means we have of passing on information: speech and images.

> Words and expressions are our way of sharing information. Any other symbols we use, for example, pictures, often have to be spoken about, that is, put into words, to make sure the other person accepts the same symbolic meaning as ourselves.

 A *Comprehending God*

God in picture form

Some people try to convey their idea of God using pictures. The difficulty here is that often people end up explaining their picture using words, so they are back to the start. For some religions, notably Islam and Judaism, it is an offence (an insult to God) to attempt to capture God in any way, even in the representational forms of much art.

Look at the following pictures and say what you think are the good points and the bad points of each attempt to show God.

B   *The nature of God?*

Summary

You should now know that human words cannot express much about the unlimited God, but words are all humans have to use about God. Some people prefer to show God through images, but these are also limited and can be misleading.

Activities

1. Draw a picture to represent God (note: not your idea of God, but God himself). How easy is this task? Why? If you do not think it is acceptable to attempt this task, explain your reasons.

2. Can you think of anything you can do or say that will help other people have an idea of your understanding of God? Explain your answer.

3. Is it better to use words or drawings when trying to communicate an idea of God? Is there any difference in your responses to using words or drawings? Explain your answer.

2.2 God in one form

God in one form

Most religions have a belief in one God. However, this apparently simple statement hides a great range of understanding about the nature of God and the way God is presented in different cultures and in different religions.

Judaism

- The Jewish people were the first to accept the idea that there is only one God.
- For Jews, the name of God is so holy that it is never written down in its completed **form** and never spoken by human beings.
- God cannot be limited in any way and this includes his title.

Beliefs and teachings

In the book of Exodus when Moses asks God for his name, God says:

God said to Moses, 'I am who I am. This is what you are to say to the Israelites: "I AM has sent me to you."'

Exodus 3:14

'I AM' is not a name, but it is a definition of God rather than a description of him. 'I AM' is basically saying that God is self-sufficient he does not need anything else.

- For Jews God cannot be shown in any figurative form (such as paintings or statues) as this would be to limit God.

Islam

- For Muslims, the oneness of God is an essential feature of their religion.
- The Muslim statement of faith is: 'There is no God but Allah' (the Shahada).
- Muhammad taught that there cannot be any division of God into separate or competing beings.
- For Muslims, God is so different to our experience as humans that it is wrong to try to portray God in any way, such as in pictures, statues or drama. Any attempt to put God into a drawn form would give a false idea of the nature of God.
- Muslims also believe that it is wrong to decorate the mosque with drawings of any living thing as it could lead people to forget that Allah is the creator, the one to be worshipped. Only geometric patterns are allowed as decorations in the mosque as these designs do not try to represent any particular thing.

Objectives

Examine different presentations of the idea of God as one.

Understand what these different ideas are trying to show about God.

Evaluate the benefits of speaking about God as one.

Research activity

Choose any two of the three monotheist religions referred to on these pages. Use the internet and/or a library to find quotes from those religions other than those already referred to on these pages that stress the idea that God is one.

Key terms

Forms: the different ways in which people picture God.

A *Blue Mosque ceiling in Istanbul, Turkey*

Christianity

- Christians also believe that there is only one God. However, this God has revealed himself to the world and has entered into humanity in the person of Jesus. The Christian understanding of the nature of God says that there are three persons in one God: God the Father, God the Son and God the Holy Spirit.

- For Christians the idea of the Trinity (three persons in one God) is a way of stating that God is both absolute and relational; that within the Godhead itself there is a relationship.

- For Christians God is dynamic and involved, not a distant, uninvolved power.

- Since God the Son became human and appeared in a limited form, some Christians do not have any problems with representing Jesus as a human being. Following on from this, these Christians find no harm in painting God the Father as an old man in the sky or the Holy Spirit as a dove. These Christians do not believe that this is exactly what God is, but they feel these images help them understand something about the nature of God.

- Other Christians believe that they should not make images of God as it leads to idolatry, which is condemned in the Ten Commandments.

B   *An early image showing the Trinity*

Summary

You should now know that many religions stress the absolute nature of God by insisting that God is one. Christians believe that God is one, but that within this Godhead there is a Trinity of persons, which makes God relational.

Study tip

Try to make clear in your own mind the differences between the Islamic idea of one God and the Christian idea of a Trinity of persons in one God – it is not easy but it is worth the effort! However, you will not be asked to talk about this comparison in the exam.

Activities

1. What ideas about the (Christian) Trinity can you get from this picture?

2. Why do you think Muslims refuse to allow anyone to produce a picture that claims to represent Allah?

3. 'It is better not to limit God by using words or images.' Do you agree? Give reasons for your answer, showing that you have thought about more than one point of view.

4. What do you think about John's views? Explain your answer.

Case study

John is a 35 year old technician who believes there is a God but who is not committed to any one religion. He says: 'For me, there can only be one God. It does not make sense to talk about there being more than one infinite object, and God must be infinite if he exists at all. However, God cannot be a remote figure who has nothing to do with his creation. If God made things he must keep them in existence and be able to relate to them.'

2.3   God in many forms

God in many forms

As seen in the previous section, God is often portrayed as one. However, there is another way of looking at the nature of God and this is by representing God according to a variety of characteristics or attributes.

Many people misunderstand this way of showing God. They would claim that these believers worship many gods (note the use of the lower case 'g' for gods that do not have the absolute power of the one God). However, the truth is that most worshippers focus on one aspect of God that they find most appealing to themselves, without denying that all the other aspects of God exist and are important. In many ways what is being acknowledged here is that humans cannot grasp the whole nature of God, so in some ways it is better to restrict their efforts to understand a limited aspect of God that they can more comfortably deal with.

Hinduism

- Most Hindus would say that there is only one God: Brahman. However, they acknowledge that Brahman can be seen in many forms.
- For Hindus the relational aspect of God can be seen in two main ways:
  - **a** in a two-pole idea, for example, good and bad that are related in the God
  - **b** in a greater complexity like the Trimurti.
- The Trimurti is Brahma (the creator god), Vishnu (the sustainer god) and Shiva (the destroyer god).
- Each of these gods shows different parts of the nature of the Brahman.
- Connected with each of these male gods is a female counterpart: Saraswati, Lakshmi and Durga; each of whom has an area of life that she is most associated with, for example, music, education.
- Other Gods such as Ganesha and Hanuman are also connected with important areas of life and celebrations.
- Hindus relate to that aspect of the Brahman that means most to them, without denying the other aspects.

Objectives

Examine the ways in which God can be shown in many forms.

Understand why presenting God in this way can be helpful to human beings.

Evaluate whether seeing God in many forms is the best way to represent God.

Research activity

Choose any four gods mentioned in Hinduism and use the internet and/or a library to examine how they are portrayed both in writing and in art.

Activity

1   As a group of 3 or 4, make a wall display that shows all the characteristics of God that are presented through the Hindu gods.

A   *The Hindu deity, Ganesha*

B   *Figures of gods in a Hindu temple*

Activity

2   What do the statues in Picture **B**, from a Hindu temple, suggest about Hindu beliefs in God?

Other religions

It is impossible to go through every religion in the world to show whether the believers accept that God is in one form or many. However, there are certain elements that were important in the earlier forms of religion. Many gods were associated with elements that controlled people's lives, such as the sun, weather, etc. It would be wrong to think that these believers worshipped the sun itself. Rather, they recognised that the power that controlled these forces could affect their lives and so they responded to these forces.

What do all these beliefs have in common?

Believers present their understanding of God in either words or images. Everyone is attempting to do the same thing: make sense of something that cannot be limited. The underlying ideas about God held by most religions have a lot of elements in common. Those who insist on the oneness of God are trying to show how God is totally different from creation and humanity. Those who try to show God in many forms are trying to show that there are many different aspects to God; none of which can really do justice to the one God but which, when taken together, can give a believer a good insight into the nature of God.

Extension activity

Choose a religion that is not mentioned in this book and use the internet and/or a library to examine how it portrays the nature of God in its writings and art.

Activities

3   Give three reasons why some people say it is best to stress that God is in one form alone.

4   Give three reasons why some people say it is best to stress that God is in many forms.

5   'It does not matter whether a believer sees God as being in one or in many forms.' Do you agree? Give reasons for your answer, showing that you have thought about more than one point of view.

Summary

You should now know that some people portray God in many forms as it makes it easier for them to deal with what is unlimited. These different forms are often different aspects of the one God, not usually believed to be different gods.

Words used about God

Common words used about God

People use words all the time to pass on information and ideas. Without words this would not be possible. However, believers say that God cannot be limited by words and this creates a problem: how can a believer speak in a meaningful way about God without, at the same time, giving the totally wrong idea about God?

The most common way to talk about God is to use common images and ideas that are based on human experience and life. When these words are used most believers accept that there is an underlying message: God in some ways is like this, but he is not exactly this. A parallel case might be found in referring to a dog as obedient. A dog might do many things that the owner asks of it, but since a dog does not have the free will a human being has, is it right to use a word such as 'obedient' about a dog? People accept the fact that the word 'obedient' is being used in a different way about the dog than it would be used about a human being, but there is an overlap of an idea that does not make it wrong to use the word 'obedient' about the dog.

Three common words used in this way by some religions are: he, Father, King.

Objectives

Examine what words are used about God and why these words are used.

Assess the meaning of the masculine, especially 'He', when used about God.

Evaluate the usefulness of masculine words when used about God.

Study tip

In this section try to look at a range of words and see what each word would imply about God. Ask yourself whether these ideas by themselves are enough to describe God.

Activity

1. a. In small groups, draw up a list of reasons that 'he' is a good word to use about God. Then do a list of reasons why 'he' is a bad word to use about God.
   b. Now do the same for 'Father' and 'King'.
   c. Choose three other words used about God and do the same task for those words.
   d. What problems has this task raised? Do you think there are any solutions to these problems? Explain your answer.

'He'

Many people question whether it is right to use a masculine word about God.

In many early societies God was thought of in terms of a man because the man was the strong protector and the provider. However, there were also many societies whose major God was described in female terms, especially as the mother fertility goddess. The dominant Western religions now have come through religions that focused on God as Father, particularly from Judaism. In Hinduism, each of their main male gods has a female goddess as consort so they should be seen as a pair rather than as separate gods.

Most religions have addressed God as he for so long that most believers automatically think of God as male, not realising that their idea of God is actually limiting God. However, people find it easier to deal with an idea of God that they can easily relate to. The fact that these ideas are supported in their holy books (for example, the Bible for Christians) and have been passed on down the ages just reaffirms most people's views of God as male.

In many languages, including English, there are three genders: masculine (usually used about males), feminine (usually used about females) and neuter (usually used about objects). In English, the pronouns used for these genders are: 'he', 'she' and 'it'.

When talking about God most people would say it would be wrong to use the word 'it' about God, as it implies something that cannot have a relationship or that cannot respond, and one of the great beliefs about God is that God cares for people.

Therefore, we are left with the choice of 'he' and 'she'. In most languages, the feminine form ('elles' in French, 'ellas' in Spanish, etc.) is only used when the group is exclusively female. If there is a mixture of male and female the masculine form is always used. This does not imply that the masculine (or male) is more important, but that the group is not exclusively female. In many ways the masculine is the 'default setting'. For many people, to use 'she' about God would raise more problems than using 'he' does. People want to focus on the real personality that is in God, on God's ability to have a relationship and to respond. Therefore, they want to use a pronoun that stresses the relationship element. Some people try to get around this problem by only using the word 'God', never using a pronoun, but this can make sentences very stilted and heavy.

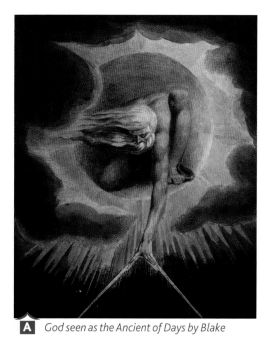

A   *God seen as the Ancient of Days by Blake*

Summary

You should now understand that we have to use words to talk about God as we have nothing else that will work. Many religions call God 'he' or use masculine words about Him as the traditional idea of God's power is connected with male qualities.

Activity

2   Write a paragraph about God that does not use the word "he" about God. How difficult did you find this task? Explain your answer. can you think of any way round the issues this task raised?

Activities

3   'It is wrong to use the word "he" about God.' Do you agree? Give reasons for your answer, showing that you have thought about more than one point of view.

4   Give five reasons why it might be good to use the word 'she' about God.

Activity

5   What is picture A trying to show about God? Do you think it succeeds in what it is trying to do? Explain your answer.

Extension activity

Use the internet and/or a library to find a poem or a piece of writing that refers to God and examine how the writer uses words to talk about God.

More words used about God: Father

Uses of the word 'Father' for God in sacred texts

The Jewish Bible

The idea of God as Father has a very long history. In the Jewish Bible (the Old Testament) we find these words said by God in the Book of Hosea:

Beliefs and teachings

[1]When Israel was a child, I loved him, and out of Egypt I called my son … [3]It was I who taught Ephraim to walk, taking them by the arms; … [4]I led them with cords of human kindness, with ties of love; I lifted the yoke from their neck and bent down to feed them.

Hosea 11:1, 3, 4

There are many examples in the Jewish Bible of God being referred to explicitly as Father. For example:

Beliefs and teachings

But you are our Father,
though Abraham does not know us
or Israel acknowledge us;
you, O Lord, are our Father,
our Redeemer from of old is your name.

Isaiah 63:16

The Jewish people and their King are often referred to as the sons of God, as in Psalm 2:7:

Beliefs and teachings

I will proclaim the decree of the Lord:
He said to me, 'You are my Son;
today I have become your Father.

Psalms 2:7

This relationship builds up throughout the Jewish history and their Bible, with the Jews recognising the caring love that God shows everyone.

The Christian Bible

Christians follow the example of Jesus who regularly addressed God as Father. Common examples of this use are:

Beliefs and teachings

[25]At that time Jesus said, 'I praise you, Father, Lord of heaven and earth, because you have hidden these things from the wise and learned, and revealed them to little children. [26]Yes, Father, for this was your good pleasure. [27]All things have been committed to me by my Father. No one knows the Son except the Father, and no one knows the Father except the Son and those to whom the Son chooses to reveal him.'

Matthew 11:25–27

Objectives

Consider words that are used about God and why these words are used.

Assess the meaning of the word 'Father' when used about God.

Evaluate the usefulness of the word 'Father' when used about God.

Activities

1. In what ways is God here referred to as a Father?
2. Do you find this use of the image of God as a Father helpful? Explain your answer.

Activity

3. Can you think of any reasons why a people such as the Jewish people might find the idea of God as Father useful? Explain your answer.

Beliefs and teachings

He went away a second time and prayed, 'My Father, if it is not possible for this cup to be taken away unless I drink it, may your will be done.'

Matthew 26:42

Beliefs and teachings

Jesus called out with a loud voice, 'Father, into your hands I commit my spirit.' When he had said this, he breathed his last.

Luke 23:46

This use of the term Father by Jesus showed that he thought of a very close, personal relationship with God. However, for Jesus this relationship was not just a private one but one he calls his followers to share.

Beliefs and teachings

For the pagans run after all these things, and your heavenly Father knows that you need them.

Matthew 6:32

This is best shown in the way Jesus tells his followers to pray:

Beliefs and teachings

'This, then, is how you should pray: "Our Father in heaven, hallowed be your name …"'

Matthew 6:9

Here the Aramaic term used is 'Abba' which is much better translated as 'daddy'. The relationship is not just personal; it is intimate and childlike.

Uses of the word 'Father' for God in other religions

Most religions share this sense of an intimate relationship with God as Father. The term implies the one who is involved in the creation of the individual, but also the provider, the one who cares and watches over the child, the one who responds in a two-way relationship (an aspect that is much better shown by the translation 'daddy' than by the more austere 'Father').

Research activity

Look in the Bible for five other occasions when the word Father is used about God. Explain what point is being made about God on these occasions.

Study tip

Think of your own image of a father and compare your idea with what believers are trying to convey using the word 'Father' about God.

A *'God holds me in his hand'*

Activities

4 Explain the differences between the words 'daddy' and 'Father'. Which word do you think is better used for God? Explain your answer.

5 Draw a picture or a series of pictures that reflect the fatherly qualities believers are trying to capture when they use the word 'Father' about God. If you think that this exercise is not a proper thing to do because of your beliefs, explain why you think this.

Summary

You should now understand that 'Father' is often seen as a good word to use to show a deep relationship with God: a being that believers think cares deeply for them.

2.6 More words used about God: King

God referred to as 'King' in sacred texts

The Jewish Bible

The idea of God as King belongs very much to earlier times when people were used to being ruled by a king. Throughout the Jewish Bible there are references to the Lord as the King. For example:

> ❝ *The Lord reigns, let the earth be glad;*
> *let the distant shores rejoice.* ❞
>
> *Psalms* 97:1

> ❝ *The Lord, the King of Israel, is with you;*
> *never again will you fear any harm.* ❞
>
> *Zephaniah* 3:15

The Christian Bible

In the Christian New Testament, the image of God and of Jesus as King occurs at important points. At the crucifixion in Luke's Gospel we find:

> ❝ [42]*Then he (the thief) said, 'Jesus, remember me when you come into*
> *your kingdom.'* [43]*Jesus answered him, 'I tell you the truth, today you will be*
> *with me in paradise.'* ❞
>
> *Luke* 23:42–43

Jesus accepts the title King for himself at the trial before Pilate when the conversation goes as follows:

> ❝ [36]*Jesus said, 'My kingdom is not of this world. If it were, my servants*
> *would fight to prevent my arrest by the Jews. But now my kingdom is from*
> *another place.'*
>
> [37]*'You are a king, then!' said Pilate.*
> *Jesus answered, 'You are right in saying I am a king. In fact, for this reason I*
> *was born, and for this I came into the world, to testify to the truth. Everyone*
> *on the side of truth listens to me.'* ❞
>
> *John* 18:36–37

In the Book of Revelations, God is regularly shown as the one who sits on the throne:

> ❝ *He who was seated on the throne said, 'I am making everything*
> *new!' Then he said, 'Write this down, for these words are trustworthy and*
> *true.'* ❞
>
> *Revelation* 21:5

Objectives

Consider words that are used about God and why these words are used.

Assess the meaning of the word 'King' when used about God.

Evaluate the usefulness of the word 'King' when used about God.

Research activity

Look in the Bible for five other occasions when the word King or Kingdom is used about God. Explain what point is being made about God on these occasions.

Extension activity

Use the internet and/or a library to research three kings who have a reputation for being good monarchs. What made them good? What might these examples show about why the word 'King' is a good word to use for God?

What does the use of 'king' about God mean?

The role of the king was to:

- protect his people
- to govern them
- to lead them in battle against the enemy
- to be obeyed.

These qualities can all find a parallel in the role of God. He is the one who guides and protects his people. He is the one who leads his people against the enemy, often shown as the power of evil. God is the one who lays down the laws that have to be obeyed. In societies that were ruled by a good king, the idea of God as the perfect king could easily be accepted. Indeed, many kings saw themselves as God's representative on earth, so the image of God as King had a strong political role to play as well as a symbolic role.

In Islam, the word 'king' itself is not used about Allah. However, the underlying idea is contained in some of the 99 Beautiful Names. The names Absolute Ruler, Governor, Majestic One, Guardian and Bestower of Honour, all reflect some of the functions of a king.

Nowadays, very few countries are ruled by a monarch who exercises real power on his/her own, so few people can really understand the depth that this image has when applied to God. Few people would be happy to use terms such as 'President' or 'Prime Minister' about God, so they keep the word and image of 'King' even though they do not fully understand the word.

A *The Judgement of Solomon. In what ways does this picture show the role of a king?*

Discussion activity

As a class, debate the topic: 'The word "King" means nothing to people in the 21st century so it should no longer be used about God.'

Activities

1. Write a list of the good points and bad points about using the word 'King' about God.
2. 'Believers should refer to God as "President" rather than as "King".' Do you agree? Give reasons for your answer, showing that you have thought about more than one point of view.

Study tip

To get an idea of what the word really means, it might be easier to think of a king in the context of the Middle Ages rather than from the 21st century.

Summary

You should now understand that 'King' can show the idea of the powerful ruler, but also the one whose job it is to protect his people. This dual role well reflects how people think of God.

Should more inclusive words be used about God?

The problem

Many people think that the common words used about God, such as Father and King, have too many overtones. This means that people can get the wrong impression of what the words are trying to say. For instance, a lot of people have had either no real experience of a father figure or they associate a father with someone who can be drunk, violent or abusive. For them, to call God 'Father' is not a positive idea as they cannot see what good qualities are being referred to. Even if people can stretch their imaginations to include a positive image of God as Father, their everyday experience can undermine what they are trying to imagine.

In the same way, the word 'King' is old-fashioned. Not many people today live in countries that are ruled by a king. The United Kingdom has a monarch as Head of State, but the actual power is exercised by an elected government. There are a few countries where there is not a constitutional monarch, but in these countries the king is often the equivalent of a dictator and abuses his power. Neither of these parallels helps people in the 21st century to appreciate the idea of God as King.

Activity

1. Look back on your negative comments about the use of the words 'He', 'Father' and 'King' in the previous sections. Can you suggest anything else (for example, other words or phrases) that might help you pass on the right idea without the negative overtones?

Objectives

Examine whether more general terms would be better used about God.

Assess the strengths and weaknesses of the more inclusive terms when used about God.

Evaluate which words help the believer have a better understanding of God.

Study tip

In this section, think about the modern trend to use words that do not show a sexist bias, for example, 'person' instead of 'man' or 'woman'. Do you find these words more useful? Apply the same type of approach to words used about God.

Inclusive language

Inclusive language is using words that are deliberately non-sexist, especially not using masculine words and pronouns when speaking about God. The idea behind this approach is that people will not be misled by the male-dominated words and their associated ideas. Some people claim that this approach will help believers get a much clearer idea of what they want to say about God. Typical of these words are: 'parent' and 'ruler'.

'Parent'

Calling God 'Father' can produce a lot of negative feelings in some people. It can also make young children, in particular, think that God is a male. This means that they may automatically think that God is bearded, not as loving as a mother, etc. Using the word 'parent' would help people, particularly the young, focus on the loving qualities of a father and mother without all the sexist bias and baggage the term 'father' can include.

A *How might this picture help a believer to relate to God?*

Discussion activity 👥👥👥

In a small group, discuss the strengths and weaknesses of the word 'parent'. What does the word 'parent' mean to you? Would you ever call your own mother or father 'parent'? Why?/Why not?

Extension activity

Find ten examples of words that have had to be changed to be more inclusive. Explain what you feel about the need for these changes.

Activities

2   'Using the word "parent" about God would leave the believer without a relationship with God.' Do you agree? Give reasons for your answer, showing that you have thought about more than one point of view.

3   Mother Julian of Norwich, a 14th-century English mystic, referred to 'Mother Jesus'. Do you think this is a helpful phrase? Explain your answer.

'Ruler'

To overcome the problems associated with the word 'king', some people suggest using the word 'ruler' about God.

Some people think that a ruler is someone who guides, protects and lays down the law for those in his care. Since this is what God does for believers, to call God a ruler would be acceptable to many people. However, in practice most people respond to the actual type of ruler, whether it is a queen, a prime minister, a president or a dictator, much better than to the fact that that person is the ruler.

The word 'ruler' is not really a part of people's everyday vocabulary (in this sense at least). It is a word that has no personal commitment or, for most people, that does not gain any real response. The concept is too remote and vague for most people to latch onto.

B   *Should God be likened to world leaders by using the title 'ruler'?*

Case study

Frances is a 57 year old nurse. She says: 'I can see that there is a lot of good in moving away from words that are too sexist or biased in their overtones. As a nurse, I have to be very careful not to accidentally upset other people. My own inclination is to use the words I was brought up with. I find it difficult to change the habits of a lifetime. However, when I want to refer to God, maybe the more inclusive words are the best ones to use as it stops my own image of God being imposed on someone else.'

What do you think about Frances' views?

Activity

4   What do you think of when you hear the word 'ruler'? Is this a good word to use about God? Explain your answer.

Summary

You should now understand that masculine words used about God can give a very misleading impression about God. Using non-gender-specific words could get over some of these problems, however general terms, such as 'parent' and 'ruler', do not usually help people to relate to the person they are talking about.

Images

Many Muslims reject any idea of making images. A lot of this attitude goes back to the second of the Ten Commandments:

Beliefs and teachings

You shall not make for yourself an idol in the form of anything in heaven above or on the earth beneath or in the waters below.

Exodus 20:4

They believe that Allah is the creator of all that exists and that everything belongs to him. It is wrong to try to copy anything in an exact way.

Images of Allah

The rule about not making an image of anything applies particularly to Allah. God is eternal, unique and unlimited. Any attempt to capture Allah in an image is an attempt to limit God, to destroy God's true nature. This is seen as an insult not just to God himself, but also to those who worship God, as it would be implying that they worshipped something that was limited and so not worthy of worship. Allah is so holy that nothing must be done to even suggest that there is any limitation in Him.

While Muslims reject portraying God in image form, they are very happy to use beautiful calligraphy and geometric forms to decorate anything that has to do with Allah, especially the Qur'an. Allah deserves the best of all human endeavours and a lot of time and effort goes into beautifying mosques and writings that are used in worship.

Research activity

Use the internet and/or a library to research how Muslims have dealt with statues and other images. Explain why they have taken the actions that they did.

Objectives

Know why Muslims reject any attempt to put God or creatures into picture form.

Understand why Muslims prefer to use the 99 Beautiful Names for Allah.

Evaluate the usefulness of the 99 Beautiful Names.

Key terms

Eternal: without limits in time; outside time.

A   *Islamic beads used to recite the 99 Beautiful Names of Allah*

Alternatives to images of Allah: the 99 Beautiful Names

Allah is not portrayed in a physical way, but there is one special way in which Muslims show the nature of Allah in a way that humans can relate to. This is the 99 Beautiful Names of Allah. Each of these names is a quality or attribute that can be found in Allah. None of them captures the fullness of the nature of Allah, but each of them gives an insight for limited human intelligence to the oneness that is Allah. These names, themselves, are often beautifully decorated to show the majesty of the one to whom they belong. Many Muslims recite these names in a form of litany or rosary as the complete list helps humans to understand something of the fullness of Allah, but it must be stressed at all times that Allah goes far beyond any human understanding, beyond even the whole list of 99 Beautiful Names.

B   *Some of the 99 names of Allah in Arabic*

Beliefs and teachings

Allah is He, other than Whom there is no other god; Who knows both what is hidden and what can be witnessed; He is the Most Compassionate and Merciful. Allah is He, other than Whom there is no other god; the Sovereign, the One, the Source of Peace, the Guardian of Faith, the Preserver of Security, the Exalted, the Compelling, the Supreme. Glory be to God, beyond any associations. He is Allah, the Creator, the Evolver, the Bestower of Form. To Him belong the Most Beautiful Names: Whatever exists in heaven and earth declares His Praise and Glory. And He is Exalted in Power, the Wise.

Qur'an 59:22–24

And Allah's are the best Names, therefore call on Him thereby, and leave alone those who violate the sanctity of His Names; they shall be recompensed for what they did; God's alone are the attributes of perfection; invoke Him, then, by these, and stand aloof from all who distort the meaning of His attributes.

Qur'an 7:180

Activities

1   Do you think the Muslim idea of the 99 Beautiful Names of Allah is a good solution to the problem of using words about God? Explain your answer.

2   'Believers should only use words about God that show a close relationship to God.' Do you agree? Give reasons for your answer, showing that you have thought about more than one point of view.

Extension activity

Use the internet and/or a library to research ten of the beautiful Names of Allah and explain what Muslims are saying about Allah when they use each of these names.

Summary

You should now know that God cannot be limited in any picture or image form. Muslims use the 99 Beautiful Names to try to express some understanding of the fullness of the nature of Allah.

Words only used about God (1)

The problem with normal words

God is so far beyond anything that the human mind can understand. This means that no normal word can do justice to the nature of God. Many people use common words, such as Father, to talk about God. However, they need to bear in mind that these words are not being used in their normal way. People often forget this, which leads to the problems that have already been noted. However, people still need to be able to talk about God, because without using words, they could say nothing at all about God.

A number of words have been developed to help people talk about God by acting as a reminder of how different God is to other beings. These words include: **all-powerful**, **all-loving**, all-knowing, all-compassionate, all-merciful. Each of these words has a special focus but there is also a lot of overlap between the ideas they contain. No one word can do justice to the full nature of God. However, it must always be remembered that these words are human inventions and so the ideas they contain are limited.

Objectives

Examine why there is a problem with using normal words about God.

Understand why all-powerful and all-loving have been made up to describe God.

Evaluate the usefulness of these words for believers.

Study tip

Think about the different implications of the words powerful, loving and all-powerful and all-loving. What are these words trying to say?

Activities

1. Explain why there is a problem with using normal words to describe God.
2. Can words invented by people overcome the problem raised by using normal words? Explain your answer.

All-powerful

To say God is all-powerful (omnipotent) means that God can do anything. This immediately raises a problem with some people as they make statements such as: 'God cannot make a square circle'. While this is true it does not show that God is limited. A square circle is a contradiction; it just cannot exist. God cannot make a square circle, not because he is limited in power, but simply because the thing cannot be made. There are many other examples like this.

It is better to think that God is the source of all being; nothing can exist without him and he can do all things. Some people question whether the existence of evil proves that God is not all-powerful. A simple answer to this is that God allows humans freedom and so limits the exercise of his own power. This is not a limitation on God.

Key terms

All-powerful: God can do anything that can be done; there is nothing outside Gods ability.

All-loving: God creates all things in his loving and caring nature so there is nothing outside concern.

Discussion activities ●●●

1. In pairs, think of five things that God cannot do. Exchange lists with another group and work out if the list produced by the other group shows any limits on God's power.
2. 'God is not all-powerful as he cannot do certain things.' Do you agree? Give reasons for your answer, showing that you have thought about more than one point of view.

∞ links

For more about how God allows humans freedom, see Chapter 4 on the problem of evil.

All-loving

By calling God all-loving (benevolent) believers are stating that God cares for his creation. One definition of love would be wanting the good of the other person. If God is loving, then he wants to express this love. God's creation is the way that God shares his love. Creation is an outward expression of God's self-giving. This self-giving in God cannot be restricted, otherwise it would show a limitation in God. Therefore, believers say that God is all-loving; that is, God is totally self-giving.

Research activity 🔍

Find two examples of people who have used or misused their power. In what way might these examples help or hinder the idea of God as a powerful being?

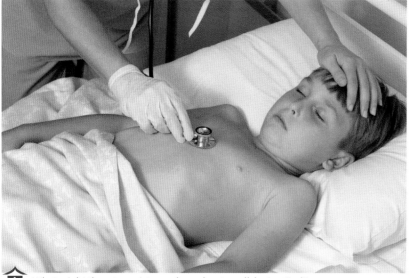

A *What might these two pictures show about an all-loving God?*

Activities

3   List six ways in which your parents show their love to you. How might the total love of God go beyond the way your parents express their love for you?

4   'It is not possible for human beings to imagine an all-loving God.' Do you agree? Give reasons for your answer, showing that you have thought about more than one point of view.

Jim is a 35 year old father of three. He says: 'To call God all-loving makes great sense to me. I know what my children mean to me and I can feel the warmth of their love in return. I can use my human love as the foundation of my understanding of the nature of God. I can never get anywhere near the loving nature of God in the way I live myself, but I can start from this to give me some real insight into what true love means.'

What do you think of Jim's views?

Case study

Summary

You should now understand that God cannot be limited and normal words suggest that he can be limited. Words such as all-powerful and all-loving try to suggest that God is without limits; however, the human mind finds it difficult to deal with these unlimited words.

Basing descriptions of God on normal human experience

People use words about God that are based on normal human experience. People understand ideas such as knowledge, compassion and mercy because they experience these qualities regularly in their lives. By using the word with 'all' as a prefix, what people are saying is that these qualities find their fullest meaning in God and, therefore, they are able to understand these aspects of God.

All-compassionate

All-compassionate is one of the 99 Beautiful Names of Allah in Islam. It also expresses a central understanding of God shared by most religions. Consider the following points.

- 'Compassion' comes from the Latin words meaning 'to suffer with', and a compassionate God is aware of human weaknesses and is concerned for the problems that these weaknesses create for people.
- A compassionate person shares with and supports another who is in need.
- The idea of the all-compassionate God is that God is involved in what is happening to the individual.
- However, in the same way that a loving parent will not interfere when their grown-up children make mistakes because they respect their children's freedom, so God will not force people to do one thing rather than another, though God does lead people if they follow his guidance.

Objectives

Examine how other words are used about God.

Understand the strengths and weaknesses of these words when they are used to describe God.

Evaluate the usefulness of these words for believers.

Key terms

All-compassionate: one of the qualities of God, showing concern for the suffering of others; literally 'suffering with'.

All-knowing: God knows everything that there is to be known.

All-merciful: a quality of God that stresses God's willingness to forgive the wrongdoer.

The Truth: the Sikh name for God showing that God is perfect and without any deceptions.

A *Can these photographs give you any idea about the nature of God?*

All-knowing

All-knowing (omniscient) implies that God is fully aware of all that happens, that nothing is beyond his awareness. Consider the following points.

- There is nothing a human being can do that God is not aware of.
- However, many people believe that this could be a limit to human freedom, the great gift that God has given people so that they can choose either for or against God.
- Some people believe that God limits his knowledge of the future so that people can be free to shape the future.
- However, these people would also say that God is intimately involved in the present, that he is fully aware of all the decisions that people freely make.

All-merciful

All-merciful is another one of the 99 Beautiful Names of Allah in Islam. It expresses a central understanding of God shared by most religions. Consider the following points.

- Mercy is a willingness to let people off for what they have done wrong.
- However, true mercy is tempered by justice.
- Justice often demands that when people have wilfully hurt others then they have to be punished.
- This punishment, however, takes into account human weakness and is prepared to put the past behind and move forward with a clean slate.
- All-mercifulness is an expression of God's all-loving nature.

The Truth

In Sikhism the belief in the oneness of God is essential. Consider the following points.

- The Ik Onkar, the Sikh statement of faith, starts off by saying: 'One Universal Creator God, The Name Is Truth'.
- The only name that can truly fit God according to Sikhism is **The Truth**, the changeless, ultimate reality, which is a pure description of God.
- The truth cannot be divided or changed in any way and because of this The Truth is thought of as the best reflection of the nature of God.

Summary

You should now know that words such as 'all-knowing', 'all-merciful', etc. can only suggest some aspects of the nature of God. People experience a weaker form of these ideas in everyday life and extend the ideas to talk about God.

Activities

1. Explain in your own words what 'all-knowing' means about God.
2. Think about how well your parents know you. Does this mean that they are stopping you doing what you want? Explain your answer.
3. Can humans be really free if God knows everything? Explain your answer.

Activities

4. Give three examples of humans showing compassion. In what ways might these examples help a believer to understand God as all-compassionate?
5. 'Humans show more compassion than God does when people suffer.' Do you agree? Give reasons for your answer, showing that you have thought about more than one point of view.

Activities

6. Draw up two examples of a person (for example, a judge or a teacher) being merciful. What shows that they are being merciful?
7. Could God be fully merciful without also being fully just? Explain your answer.

Activities

8. Explain why Truth is seen as an absolute idea.
9. 'The Truth is the best phrase to use about God.' Do you agree? Give reasons for your answer, showing that you have thought about more than one point of view.

2.11 Words that show God's closeness and distance

Transcendent

When the word '**transcendent**' is used about God, the focus is on God being totally beyond any created thing.

- God is outside creation and God is not limited in any way, unlike all created things.
- Everything depends on God, but God is not dependent on any other thing.
- We know that the universe is made up of billions of galaxies like our own, but our limited minds cannot imagine the extent of this universe. The idea of the transcendent God is that God is greater than the whole of the universe.
- This idea does not suggest that God is physical, but that he is the creator of all that is: physical things as well as non-physical things.

It is easier to think of transcendent as meaning God goes far beyond the whole of all that exists.

Immanent

While the word 'transcendent' looks at the macrocosm (the whole of the universe as one thing), the word '**immanent**' deals with the microcosm (each little bit that makes up the whole).

- In the Jewish and Christian scriptures there is the idea that God is more intimately involved with the individual than the person's own breath.
- God is the foundation of my being, the one who keeps me in existence from second to second.

This close connection with God as the source of every person's life can be both frightening and supportive for the believer:

- It is frightening because it is difficult to think of a being who is more involved in my own existence than I am.
- It is supportive because it means that I am known by God in a way that goes far beyond my understanding and yet which must mean that I am understood.

Objectives

Examine what the words transcendent, immanent, personal and impersonal mean.

Understand what these words are trying to convey about the nature of God.

Evaluate the usefulness of these ideas when they are used about God.

Activities

1. Put in your own words the difference between transcendent and immanent. Try to use an example to help your explanation.

2. Why do you think the writer has used phrases such as, 'God is the foundation of **my** being' rather than talking impersonally when he was writing about immanent?

3. 'God is too remote to be thought of as immanent.' Do you agree? Give reasons for your answer, showing that you have thought about more than one point of view.

Personal

The idea of a **personal** God flows from the idea of an immanent God. Personal means that God is involved with, and cares for, everything about each individual.

- God is not thought of exclusively as a remote being but as a being who is deeply concerned in each person's life.
- This greatly increases the importance of each person, created and loved uniquely by God.
- It also stresses the limitless character of God. God is so great that every little part of creation is important to him.

A   *What does this picture suggest about God as transcendent?*

B   *God is intimately involved in life. He is personal*

Impersonal

The opposite idea of personal is **impersonal**.

- God is not affected by what any individual does; he is remote in that sense.
- This shows that both the closeness and concern of God in my life and the fact that God exists regardless of me are valid ideas.
- The idea of God as impersonal stops any idea of God being limited by relations with individuals.

Activities

4 In pairs draw up three differences between personal and impersonal. You might find it helpful to use examples.

5 'It is easier to think of God as impersonal rather than personal.' Do you agree? Give reasons for your answer, showing that you have thought about more than one point of view.

Summary

You should now understand the belief that God is outside the whole of creation and is greater than the whole of creation. He is not changed by anything. However, God is intimately involved in the individual's life in a personal, caring way.

2

The characteristics of God – summary

For the examination you should now be able to:

✓ understand the significance of God in one or many forms

✓ understand and evaluate the type of language used about God, including Truth, Father, King he and The Eternal and the more inclusive terms such as parent and ruler

✓ know and understand the significance of other words for God including all-powerful, all-loving, all-knowing, all-compassionate, all merciful and transcendent, immanent, personal and impersonal

✓ appreciate the strengths and weaknesses of all these ways of talking about God.

Sample answer

1 Write an answer to the following exam question:

'It would be better to refer to God as parent rather than as Father.'

Do you agree? Give reasons for your answer, showing that you have thought about more than one point of view.

(6 marks)

2 Read the following sample answer.

> In many religions, God is presented as Father either directly or through images. Christians follow Jesus who called God 'Father' according to the Gospels and he taught his followers to call God 'daddy' or 'abba'. This shows that Jesus had a special relationship with God that he wanted other people to share. This is very similar to the way Jews often use the image of a protective, loving God so they see God as acting as a father even when they do not use that title about him. Humans respond well to the idea of a loving father because it shows an intimate relationship.
>
> Some people would argue that 'Father' removes all the loving, motherly qualities that can also be found in God and that understanding the word 'father' in the way that is necessary to understand God means that you have to have a good relationship with your own father, which does not always happen. They would say 'parent' deals with both these issues, but I think that 'parent' is too remote a word. I never use it about my mum and dad, so why should it have any meaning for me when I use it about God?

3 With a partner, discuss the sample answer. Do you think there are other things the student could have included in the answer?

4 What mark would you give this answer out of 6? Look at the mark scheme in the Introduction on page 7 (AO2). What are the reasons for the mark you have given?

Practice questions

1   Read the extract below and answer the following questions.

> 66 ¹O Lord, you have searched me
> and you know me.
>
> ²You know when I sit and when I rise; 99
> you perceive my thoughts from afar.
>
> Psalm 139:1–2

(a) Explain why the above passage is a good example of God as immanent.   *(3 marks)*

(b) In what ways would a transcendent God be different from an immanent God?   *(3 marks)*

(c) 'It is limiting to think about God as only in one form.' Do you agree?
     Give reasons for your answer, showing that you have thought about more
     than one point of view.   *(6 marks)*

Study tip   Remember the stimulus material is there to be used in your answer and can often give
you important hints. In (a) you are asked to explain why the passage is a good example, so
feel free to refer directly to what the passage says and comment on it. There are no marks,
however, if you simply rewrite the passage.

3 Revelation and enlightenment

3.1 General revelation and revelation through nature

■ Revelation

God is so much greater than the human mind can grasp that humans themselves cannot get any true idea of what God is like. This could cause a great problem as there is no really valid, external way of saying anything about God. However, believers in all religions feel that they have the right to make certain statements about God, always accepting that these statements are incomplete. The underlying approach is based on the belief that God shows or reveals himself in many ways.

The word 'reveal' is closely associated with the idea of 'unveiling' (meaning lifting a veil to show something of what God is like). God shows himself in such a way that the people can make sense of what God is telling humans about himself.

The more God reveals about himself, the more people can get to know him. Unless God does the revealing, mankind remains in the dark about what God is like. This is an important idea: if God does not let humans know something about Himself, humans have no understanding at all about God. The people who make statements about the nature of God have to accept that these statements are based on something that God has shown about himself, not on any human thoughts.

Activities

1 Explain in your own words why humans cannot begin to understand God.
2 Write three sentences using the word 'reveal'. What do these sentences show about the meaning of the word 'reveal'?

Many people divide **revelation** into two groups:

- **General revelation** that is available for anyone to respond to.
- Special revelation that takes place in a specific event or experience and is shown to one person or a small group of people.

∞ links

For a definition of special revelation see page 60.

Objectives

Examine how believers claim to see God through ways that should be open to all people.

Appreciate why people believe that nature can be seen as a way of understanding God, even though God is beyond human understanding.

Key terms

Revelation: God shows himself to believers; this is the only way anybody can really know anything about God.

General revelation: the belief that God can be known by anybody who is prepared to accept the idea that through creation, e.g. nature, God shows his true nature.

Research activity

1 Draw up a list of 10 different examples that believers would call a) general revelations and b) specific revelations.

General revelation through nature

Many people think that they can get some idea of what God is like just by looking at the different aspects of creation. It can be compared to a painting: a painting shows you a lot about the artist, his values, abilities, priorities, perception of what is around him. It is wrong to say that a painting tells you everything about an artist, as there are so many aspects of the artist's life that might not be connected with the painting. However, you can get some real insights into the painter and, the more of his work you see, the more you can appreciate how he works.

A   *What does this scene show about God?*

Believers see all creation as the work of God. It is his gift to everyone. It shows his power and his ability to create. Nature also reflects the beauty and the interdependence of everything. In the same way that a painting tells you something about the artist, so, for believers, nature tells them something about God.

There are many aspects of nature that make people wonder. The power of a strong wind, the beauty of the night sky, the vastness of the universe: all make people sit back and reflect, even if they do not believe in a creator God. For believers, these powers of nature are a pale reflection of the greatness of the God who made them. An artist cannot make something greater than himself. In the same way, nature and the vast universe are dependent on a God who is greater, but they still reflect something about their creator.

Summary

You should now understand that religious believers can only know the things that God reveals about himself. They have no other knowledge of God. Nature can show some of God's qualities, just as a painting shows something about an artist.

Activities

3   Choose a piece of music, a poem or a picture. What does this piece of music/ poetry/picture tell you about the composer/writer/ artist?

4   Think of an occasion when you did something and a stranger told you off. What does that person's behaviour show you about them? Is that all there is to that person? Do you fully understand that person? Explain your answer.

Research activity

2   Choose one natural event on Earth or in the Solar System or in the Universe. Use the internet and/or a library to find out about the event you have chosen and write a detailed description. What might a believer say this event shows about the creator (accepting for the moment that there is a creator)?

Activity

5   'Humans only need to look at nature to get a clear idea of what God is like.' Do you agree? Give reasons for your answer, showing that you have thought about more than one point of view.

Believers think that human beings are the most important part of God's creation. In the Book of Genesis it says:

> 66 *So God created man in his own image, in the image of God he created him; male and female he created them.* 99
>
> *Genesis 1:27*

Objectives

Examine how believers claim to see God through the ways that other people live their lives.

Appreciate why people believe that human lives and behaviour can be seen as ways of understanding God, even though God is beyond human understanding.

Evaluate the different arguments about general revelation.

This statement claims that human beings share in the qualities of God. Humans have gifts and abilities that other parts of creation lack. While grass and trees can be very beautiful and useful for life to continue, especially as food for the animals, it is the human race that is able to think, to love, to discover, to reflect on what life is all about. Since this is the case, believers would claim that they can discover something about the nature of God by looking at the way human beings react in positive ways. These qualities must come from the creator; they cannot just have appeared of their own accord. Many people would argue that, just as humans cannot make a computer that is more human than themselves, so the qualities that are found in God's creatures (human beings) must be lesser than God's own qualities. These qualities must find their perfect expression in God.

Human love is a pale reflection of God's love. Love might be difficult to define, but it is easy to see it in action. There are many examples:

- The willingness of a mother to put her children's needs before her own shows true love in action.
- The way some people are prepared to go abroad and to spend years in squalid conditions trying to improve the lives of poor people rather than simply having a comfortable life in their own country is inspiring.
- The way some people, such as Maximilian Kolbe, Mahatma Gandhi and the Dalai Lama are prepared to give up their own lives and even die to help other people shows a true quality that cannot be explained without some reference to an ultimate source of values: God.

For believers, these people share in the loving nature of God and they help people to appreciate what God is like.

A *How might this act show something about God?*

Research activity 🔍

Research how one person has put the needs of other people before their own, for example by going to work abroad with aid relief or working to bring justice and equality to the oppressed e.g. Martin Luther King. How might a believer use this person's actions as a way of showing what God is like?

There are many ultimate values that need to have some origin outside human existence:

- Truth cannot have any limits. People are prepared to live by the truth and die for it. They are not prepared to compromise on certain standards that might compromise the truth as far as they are concerned.

- Forgiveness means being able to let go of any hurt done and to put the past behind you and give everybody a new start. The aim of forgiveness is not to gain anything special for the person who makes the first move, and yet it is seen as one of the greatest qualities that humans possess. Again this reflects God's qualities.

- Justice means accepting that there needs to be some balance in life: that those who have offended need to make some type of recompense. Yet most people accept that justice should be tempered by love. In this many believers feel that they are expressing the true nature of God in their own lives.

These qualities are without limits and so must also belong to the nature of God.

B　*Can human beings share the qualities of God?*

Case study

Matthew is a 30 year old solicitor. He says: 'When I was at college, a friend of mine called Greg decided to finish off his college life by going to do a year's voluntary service overseas. He said that he had been helped through school and college and wanted to do something in return by helping others. I thought at the time that he was mad, throwing away a really good career prospect, even for a year, just to live in squalor. He went and spent six years there. When he came back home last summer I saw a great change in him. Everything he did was done in a committed yet gentle way. He gave people time and never held anything against anybody, no matter how offensive they were. It made me realise that God must be very like this in his character, though obviously much greater than any human being. I found out about God through Greg.'

Activities

1　Think of three people in different types of occupation. What qualities does each of these people use to do his/her job properly? How might these qualities show something about the nature of God?

2　'It is easier to understand God through nature than it is through other people.' Do you agree? Give reasons for your answer, showing that you have thought about more than one point of view.

Summary

You should now understand the belief that humans are created by God. The qualities humans show in the way they live their lives must be a reflection of the qualities that are found in God.

3.3 Special revelation: sacred texts

Special revelation

In contrast to general revelation, which is available to all people who are open to using the power of reason, there is **special revelation**. This is a specific item of information or understanding about God that cannot be worked out through reason, but has to be made known directly from God.

The most common type of special revelations are sacred texts. Typical examples of sacred texts as special revelation are:

- the Qur'an that was given to Muhammad
- the Jewish Torah
- the Vedas of Hinduism
- the Christian Bible.

To enable us to study special revelation in a more manageable way, we will first talk about sacred texts, followed by prayer and worship, visions, dreams and, finally, enlightenment.

Sacred texts

All religions have some form of **sacred text**, though each religion may place a different kind of importance on the scriptures. Most sacred texts started off as a purely oral (spoken) set of teachings that may or may not have been given in a vision or experience of God. These were passed on for years before eventually being written down.

- In Hinduism the Vedas are seen as containing the central core of Hindu beliefs and worship. Hindus believe that the Vedas have no human author, but the words were heard or seen in visions by priestly seers. They were written down when there was a fear that the meaning was being changed.

- The most important Jewish text is the Torah that includes the law passed down to Moses on Mount Sinai. This is believed to have come directly from God so many Jews follow the Torah very exactly.

- The teachings of the Buddha were collected over a long period of time in the Tripitaka and in the Sutras. They are teachings based on the experience of Gautama Siddartha, the Buddha. These scriptures do not hold the same sacred feeling that the scriptures of the other religions have.

- In Christianity, the Bible is seen as the Word of God. Christians may believe this is because God gave the words directly to people or they may believe that the writers were inspired by God to write in their own words. This applies in particular to the Gospels as these contain the actions and teachings of Jesus. All Christian teachings must be based on material in the Bible.

- For Muslims, the Qur'an is the word of Allah, revealed to Muhammad between 610 and 632 CE, recited by Muhammad and then written down. Since it is the word of Allah, everything contained in the Qur'an has great value to Muslims.

Objectives

Examine how people claim that God has revealed himself through sacred texts.

Understand different ways of interpreting these texts and what these interpretations mean for the believer.

Evaluate different interpretations of sacred texts.

Activity

1. Explain in your own words the difference between special revelation and general revelation.

Key terms

Special revelation: God shows himself to an individual or group of individuals in a specific, direct way, as opposed to general revelation.

Sacred texts: writings which are believed to originate from God or a god or are special to a religion.

Activities

2. Draw up a list of points that could be used to say why sacred texts are special.

3. 'Sacred texts have been used by believers for so long that there must be some real value in them.' Do you agree? Give reasons for your answer, showing that you have thought about more than one point of view.

■ For Sikhs, the Guru Granth Sahib (or Adi Granth) contains the teachings of the Ten Gurus as well as teachings of Hindu and Muslim writers and is treated with the same respect that would be paid to a human guru.

The six main world religions described above reflect the approach taken by believers to sacred texts. The message of the texts has to be taken very seriously as it reflects the religion's understanding of God, often based on special experiences of God by individuals or the wisdom of leaders and thinkers of the religion. They also show how God wants believers to behave.

A *The Torah*

B *The Vedas*

Summary

You should now know that believers claim that God lets them know about himself in direct, personal ways. Sacred texts or scriptures are seen as the word of God in many religions.

Extension activity

Choose one of the sacred texts discussed and do some more research on it using the internet and/or a library. You could put together your chosen text. Describe what it is, what it contains and how it is treated and followed by members of the religion.

Discussion activity

As a class, debate the topic: 'Humans are the ones that have written down the documents that are called sacred texts so they are nothing special.'

Study tip

Try to see what the different sacred texts have in common and how they are respected by believers. Do not try to argue which one is correct – that is not part of this exam paper.

While most believers accept that the sacred texts come from God and have to be respected as such, there are disputes about exactly how the texts are to be understood. There are different groups within each religion and each group tends to take a different stand on the issue. For the sake of simplicity the major positions could be described as **fundamentalist** and liberal. These terms do not apply as much to Buddhism as to some of the other religions.

Fundamentalist approach

The fundamentalist approach takes the line that the text comes directly from God so can contain no error, as God would not mislead his people. Fundamentalists tend to take every part of the text seriously, if not as word-perfect. They try to live according to what is written down in the text, regardless of when the document was written or the context in which it was written. There are fundamentalist Muslims who still apply the severe punishments for theft as laid down in the Qur'an. There are fundamentalist Christians and Jews who believe Adam and Eve are historical people.

Fundamentalists do not believe that human beings can do anything other than accept that the scriptures contain the very words of God, sometimes saying that God dictated the words to humans to write down. Because of their belief in the holiness of God, they also believe that the sacred text cannot be questioned.

A *A Buddhist monk reading the Tipitaka*

Objectives

Examine different interpretations of sacred texts.

Understand how different interpretations of sacred texts might lead believers to behave differently.

Key terms

Fundamentalist: a person who believes in the basics of a religion, particularly believing that what is contained in the sacred text is an accurate, almost factual, record that cannot be questioned.

Activities

1. Give two strengths and two weaknesses of a fundamentalist approach to interpreting sacred texts.

2. Choose a passage from a sacred text and show how the text would be understood according to a fundamentalist interpretation.

Extension activity

Find a fundamentalist website on the internet and examine the reasons fundamentalists hold the views that they do.

Liberal approach

People who adopt the liberal approach would also accept that the sacred text comes from God. They have a different understanding of how this works. Most liberals see the texts as presenting insights into God, but as written down by human beings in a very specific time and social setting, so the text reflects a lasting truth presented in a way that needs to be understood differently by a different society. Many liberal Jews and Christians would no longer live by the rules governing the type of clothes to wear or the food to eat as laid down in the Bible. Many Muslims regard the punishments for law-breaking prescribed in the Qur'an as needing to be updated.

Liberals do not question the underlying truths that can be found in their scriptures, or that they were written by people inspired by God and their religious beliefs, but they do question how much a modern society should follow every word of the text written many centuries ago. They would also examine and interpret the texts to discover what the meaning is for modern life.

Other interpretations

There are some people who question the whole validity of having sacred texts. These people would take the line that the texts were written down by people who wanted to show their own understanding of God. The texts only gained value because other people accepted the message that they contained as a reflection of their own beliefs too. On this approach the 'sacred texts' are merely human products that might be totally wrong in what they say about God.

However, even if what is presented about God cannot be proved, what these texts do is give a good insight into how human beings show their understanding of faith. This common understanding might well reflect a deep human awareness of the nature of God that shows itself in the way the writers phrase things and the language they use.

B   *Reading the Qur'an*

Activity

5   'God cannot speak to believers through a text or book.' Do you agree? Give reasons for your answer, showing that you have thought about more than one point of view.

Summary

You should now know that fundamentalist believers believe that the texts contain the words of God as he gave them directly and they will not question anything that the texts contain. Liberal believers believe that the underlying message of the texts is important, but that the texts themselves were written in a specific time and setting so have to be interpreted.

Study tip

Try to examine a few texts from different scriptures and apply the different approaches. This will help you to see how much difference there is between the various groups.

Special revelation: prayer

For theists, **prayer** is an opening up of the heart and mind to God. This allows God to reveal himself to the person praying, as there is an acceptance of the presence and the reality of God. Buddhists see prayer as a practice that can enhance meditation, which helps them to gain moksha and the escape from rebirth.

Forms of prayer

Prayer can take many forms. The most common forms of prayer are listed below.

Silent prayer

Silent prayer is being still in the presence of God, being totally open to what God has to offer. Many people feel that words get in the way when they try to speak to God and this can create feelings of being ill-at-ease. Believers who are convinced that God loves them cannot accept the idea of being uneasy in the presence of God and so they simply sit at peace and let their presence express the commitment to God that words might otherwise try to convey.

Meditation

Meditation has a lot in common with silent prayer. A person who meditates tries to empty his mind from all distractions so that he can focus on God alone. This can be done by thinking of an idea or event that shows the person that God is at work in his own life or in the life of other people. The trigger to help focus can be found in the sacred books. Meditation can remove all obstacles to communication with God and can often allow a person to follow a train of thought so deeply that he can become closer to the reality that is God.

Communal prayer

This is when a group of believers come together to share prayer, often using a set format, though some believers prefer to pray in a spontaneous fashion even when they are in a group. Communal prayer can help a person who is having difficulty praying, as the others can support and give an example that enables that individual to persevere.

Liturgical prayer

This is prayer that follows a set format, usually done in a formal setting. It is often led by a minister or religious leader and people can find the same format used in many places. The Roman Catholic Mass is a typical example of liturgical prayer.

Objectives

Examine the role of prayer as a means of revelation.

Understand how prayer helps believers to respond to God.

Evaluate the need for prayer in the believer's life.

links

To find out more about moksha see page 96.

Key terms

Prayer: communicating with God through words of praise, thanksgiving or confession, or requests for help or guidance.

A *At prayer*

Repetition of a phrase

This is a very common practice. Sikhs use the Ik Onkar, Jews use the Shema, Orthodox Christians use the Jesus Prayer. All of these are short sayings that the believer repeats and that help the believer think about the central principles of faith.

Prayer through a physical posture

Many believers take a special position when they pray. This is especially true of Muslims who go through a whole series of movements during the salat, the obligatory prayer said five times a day. The movements show that the whole person is involved in the prayer.

◼ The point of prayer

Whatever form the prayer takes, it is a giving of time, part of the believer's life, to building up a relationship with God. By opening the heart and mind, the believer wants to accept all that God has to give.

All prayer is basically a statement of faith. Prayer is an acknowledgement by the believer that God not only has the desire to be involved in the believer's life, but also has the power to respond to what the believer requests. There are many different reasons for prayer. Praise, petition, intercession and sorrow are all reasons commonly used by the believer. Whatever the reason for the prayer, the believer comes closer to God.

B   *Muslims performing salat*

Study tip

If you find it hard to talk in general about prayer, think of a particular prayer that you know and examine what that is saying about the believer and about God. Then apply the same ideas to other prayers.

Activities

1. Choose two forms of prayer and explain what they are and how they might help a person to pray.
2. Explain how praise and a prayer of sorrow can help a believer to become more aware of the nature of God.
3. 'Prayer makes no difference to a believer's life.' Do you agree? Give reasons for your answer, showing that you have thought about more than one point of view.

Case study

Margaret is a 30 year old secretary who is a Christian. She says: 'I like to make time every day to pray. I feel that God is important in my life. All I can do to show this is to give some time just to be aware of him and to focus on all that he has done for me. I know that prayer does not add anything to God but it does strengthen my relationship with him. I like to compare it to phoning a friend that I cannot often see. By talking we are still close to each other and sometimes we talk just for the sake of being aware of each other. The words are not that important. The fact of talking is. With prayer, I am in the presence of God and this is one way to maintain my relationship with God.'

What do you think of Margaret's views?

Summary

You should now understand that religious believers use prayer as an opening up of the heart and mind to God, which can take many different forms. Many people use words when they pray, but many pray in silence.

3.6   Special revelation: worship

What is worship?

Worship is given to that which has worth or value in a person's life. Worship should only be given to the one of ultimate value: God. Any worship that is given to a lesser thing is called idolatry. Worship goes beyond prayer, though prayer can be included in worship. Worship can take many forms:

- Going to a temple to offer sacrifice can show the believer acknowledges the need to give God time and physical effort.
- Taking care of a shrine in the home, for example, uncovering the Guru Granth Sahib for Sikhs or putting an offering before a shrine dedicated to one or more of the Hindu gods.
- Going to the mosque on Friday or taking part in the salat five times a day is a way for Muslims to show commitment to Allah.
- Attending the synagogue on the Shabbat is an essential part of what it means to be a Jew.

All these practices show that the believer is offering their life to God.

A   *Muslims at worship in their home*

For Jews, Christians and Muslims worship can include living by the demands of God or Allah at all times. The giving of the whole life to God is the highest form of worship a believer can give.

Worship can be an individual thing or it can be done as part of a group. Sometimes the believer finds it useful to get the support of others, to feel as though they are not on their own in their awareness of God. However it is done, worship is acknowledging that God is important to the believer. As with prayer, once this commitment takes place, it is easier for the believer to become aware of the presence of God and to be open to receiving guidance from God and greater insight into the nature of God.

Objectives

Examine the role of worship as a means of revelation.

Understand how worship helps believers to respond to God.

Evaluate the need for worship in the believer's life.

Research activity

1. Choose one of the world's major religions and use the internet and/or a library to research how the believers offer private worship.

Key terms

Worship: acts of religious praise, honour or devotion.

Activities

1. Explain why worship is important for the believer.
2. 'Living by the demands of the religion is more important than worship.' Do you agree? Give reasons for your answer, showing that you have thought about more than one point of view.

How valid is worship?

Some people might argue that worship does nothing for God. If God is totally perfect, nothing human beings can do will make any difference to God. That is presuming there is such a thing as God anyway. Some people would claim that the only one who gets anything out of prayer or worship is the person who is performing the action. If the person praying is focusing on something that might not even exist, there is a possibility that that person is deluded and that any good feelings or 'messages' that they get are simply delusions. If there is no God, praying and worship will not change anything. Believers might argue that the real point of prayer and worship is to help them accept the role of God in their lives.

Those people who claim that they get a better understanding of God through prayer and worship can only present their viewpoint. Prayer and worship are essentially personal, private things, even when they are performed in public with others. What the individual experiences is unique. While that individual might gain a real sense of new awareness of God from the prayer or worship, this awareness cannot be shared with others.

Research activity O⟋

2 Choose one of the world's major religions and use the internet and/or a library to research how the believers share public worship.

B *Even in a public place, worship can be a very private thing*

Study tip

As with prayer, it is often easier to look at worship through actual examples and then look at the general principles in the light of this example.

Activities

3 Explain why some people would argue that the experience of God gained through prayer or worship cannot be shared.

4 'Prayer and worship are a waste of time.' Do you agree? Give reasons for your answer, showing that you have thought about more than one point of view.

Summary

You should now understand that worship is an acceptance that God has ultimate value in the believer's life. Believers can feel the presence of God through worship. Worship can take many forms, but they all take time and commitment.

3.7 Special revelation: visions

Visions

A **vision** is an experience that comes from outside in picture or image form. The vision usually has a deep meaning for the person receiving it. The vision enables the receiver to become aware of a reality in a new way or with a new intensity. Sometimes a few people can share the same vision, but usually the vision is seen by just one person.

Examples of visions

There are many visions referred to in the Bible. Many of the Jewish prophets experienced intense visions that gave them messages about God's dealing with the Jewish people that the prophet had to pass on. Here is an example of one of these prophetic visions and a similar kind of vision experience by a christian disciple of Jesus.

Objectives

Examine how people claim God and his message came to them in visions.

Understand how these visions can change people's lives.

Evaluate the importance of visions for believers and their faith.

Case study

Isaiah's commission

¹*In the year that King Uzziah died, I saw the Lord seated on a throne, high and exalted, and the train of his robe filled the temple. ²Above him were seraphs, each with six wings: With two wings they covered their faces, with two they covered their feet, and with two they were flying. ³And they were calling to one another: 'Holy, holy, holy is the Lord Almighty; the whole earth is full of his glory.'*

⁴*At the sound of their voices the doorposts and thresholds shook and the temple was filled with smoke.*

⁵*'Woe to me!' I cried. 'I am ruined! For I am a man of unclean lips, and I live among a people of unclean lips, and my eyes have seen the King, the Lord Almighty.'*

⁶*Then one of the seraphs flew to me with a live coal in his hand, which he had taken with tongs from the altar. ⁷With it he touched my mouth and said, 'See, this has touched your lips; your guilt is taken away and your sin atoned for.'*

⁸*Then I heard the voice of the Lord saying, 'Whom shall I send? And who will go for us?' And I said, 'Here am I. Send me!' ⁹He said, 'Go and tell this people: Be ever hearing, but never understanding; be ever seeing, but never perceiving.'*

¹⁰*Make the heart of this people calloused; make their ears dull and close their eyes. Otherwise they might see with their eyes, hear with their ears, understand with their hearts, and turn and be healed.'*

Isaiah 6:1–10

Case study

Peter's vision

For Christians there are visions recorded in the New Testament, for example:

⁹*About noon the following day as they were on their journey and approaching the city, Peter went up on the roof to pray. ¹⁰He became hungry and wanted something to eat, and while the meal was being prepared, he fell into a trance. ¹¹He saw heaven opened and something like a large sheet being let down to earth by its four corners. ¹²It contained all kinds of four-footed animals, as well as reptiles of the earth and birds of the air. ¹³Then a voice told him, 'Get up, Peter. Kill and eat.'*

¹⁴*'Surely not, Lord!' Peter replied. 'I have never eaten anything impure or unclean.'*

¹⁵*The voice spoke to him a second time, 'Do not call anything impure that God has made clean.'*

¹⁶*This happened three times, and immediately the sheet was taken back to heaven.*

Acts 10:9–16

A *Peter's vision*

Key terms

Vision: seeing something, especially in a dream or trance, that shows something about the nature of God or the afterlife.

Research activity

Look up at least one more vision in the Jewish or Christian scriptures. Either describe the vision in your own words or try to draw a picture of it.

Extension activity

Look for an account of a vision in one of the other world religions, using the internet and/or a library. How does this vision compare to the ones described from the Jewish and Christian scriptures?

Activities

1 Do you find these visions easy to accept? Why/why not?
2 Do you think Picture A reflects the vision? Explain your answer.

Summary

You should now understand that visions enable those who receive them to get a deeper insight into a part of their faith. Visions often cause people to change either their way of life or the focus of their activities.

Study tip

Look at what types of features usually occur in a vision. You do not need to have detailed knowledge of any particular vision.

3.8 Special revelation: modern visions

Modern visions

Visions have been recorded throughout history, but some are more widely accepted as genuine than others. There are also recorded visions from more recent times, for example, the appearances of the Virgin Mary at Lourdes are accepted as authentic visions by Roman Catholics.

Recognise that visions are recorded as still happening.

Evaluate the importance of visions for believers and their faith.

Case study

The vision of Bernadette

On a cold February day in 1859, a young girl called Bernadette was asked by her mother to go down to the river to collect driftwood and fallen branches for the fire. She was accompanied to the icy river by two younger children. When they got to the water, the two younger girls crossed, but Bernadette dawdled on the river bank, removing her stockings to prepare herself for crossing the river. Suddenly Bernadette heard a sound like a rush of wind. She looked around her and saw a golden cloud gradually float down from a nearby cave to reveal a beautiful young lady within it. The lady sat upon a rock and smiled at Bernadette, her eyes blue and gentle. She wore a soft white robe with a girdle of blue around her waist and her hair was partially covered by a long white veil. Bernadette's fear was calmed by the lady's beautiful smile, and she walked towards her, and then knelt in reverence. Bernadette was a religious girl, and took her rosary from her pocket to say her prayers, as she often did when she felt unsettled. The mysterious lady also produced a rosary and as Bernadette prayed, she passed the large white beads between her fingers along with her, not speaking, except to repeat the word 'Gloria' with Bernadette. When the prayers were finished, the lady and the glowing cloud around her disappeared into the cave and Bernadette was left alone. Bernadette remained kneeling, a peaceful, faraway look on her face, for some time, until the other girls returned looking for her. Seeing her kneeling they thought she had been praying to get out of the chore of gathering firewood, and scolded her. As they started on their way home, Bernadette excitedly told them what had happened, asking them not to tell anyone else about it. However, one of the girls did tell an adult that night, and soon the news spread. After this the lady appeared on another seventeen occasions.

The lady eventually told Bernadette that she was the "Immaculate Conception", a teaching about Mary that had recently been declared official by the Pope.

A *The vision of Bernadette*

Visions of the 'Three Seers'

The Blessed Virgin Mary, the Mother of God, appeared six times to three shepherd children ('the Three Seers') near the town of Fatima, Portugal between 13 May and 13 October 1917. Appearing to the children, the Blessed Virgin told them that She had been sent by God with a message for every man, woman and child living in our century. Coming at a time when civilization was torn asunder by war and bloody violence, She promised that Heaven would grant peace to all the world if Her requests for prayer, reparation and consecration were heard and obeyed.

Our Lady of Fatima explained to the children that war is a punishment for sin and warned that God would further castigate the world for its disobedience to His Will by means of war, hunger and the persecution of the Church, the Holy Father and the Catholic Faithful.

www.fatima.org/essentials/facts/story1.asp

B *The statue of Mary at Lourdes, France*

How valid are visions?

The important thing about religious visions is that they happen to an individual person. A vision is a special revelation. The vision is perceived to come from outside; it is not usually 'looked for' by the person receiving it. The weakness with all visions is that it is almost impossible to put a picture or an experience into words. Visions only have meaning if they convey a deeper message, either about God or about events, and people will try to work out their meaning and remember it. Often a vision is a startling and very memorable experience that a person will want to tell others about.

Some people would claim that visions are the result of a person's mind running wild. Some people suggest that the mind has been stimulated with drugs, alcohol or something similar and they would reject the validity of any claim made. They would argue that there was no guarantee that what was being referred to actually came from God and not just from an over-active imagination.

Study tip

You will not be examined on any particular vision, but you might find it useful to be able to talk generally about a particular vision that you have read about.

Activities

1 Read an account of a vision. Now either draw the vision or put it in your own words. Having tried to do this, explain what was easy and difficult about the activity. What might this suggest about visions and the visionary?

2 How do you think the lives of each of the people whose visions are recorded in this section were affected by their vision?

3 'Visions are only important for the person who receives them.' Do you agree? Give reasons for your answer, showing that you have thought about more than one point of view.

Summary

You should now recognise that visions are external images that convey a deeper understanding to the people who receive them. They are difficult to communicate to other people, but are seen as a special revelation if they can be interpreted to provide a message.

Dreams

Visions tend to occur when the visionary is awake and aware of their surroundings. **Dreams** tend to happen when a person is asleep. Most people have dreams. Many people forget their dreams and most dreams seem to have little explicit value. However, there are some dreams that can make a deep impression on the person dreaming and, as with visions, they might give the dreamer new insights into reality and into God. This can happen because the normal working of the mind and the control people normally have over what they are thinking about are put into suspension when people are asleep.

Because of the intensity of these experiences, few people would simply categorise these dreams along with all the other millions of dreams that occur each week. These dreams are very memorable and can give a new direction to the person's life, or give a totally new awareness of the role of God in the person's life. For these dreams to be valid, they have to be free from any artificial stimulus, for example, drugs.

Examples of dreams

Dreams are referred to in the Jewish Bible, as in the case study that follows.

Objectives

Examine how people claim God comes to them in dreams.

Evaluate the importance of dreams for believers and their faith.

Key terms

Dreams: a series of thoughts, images and sensations occurring in a person's mind during sleep.

Case study

Jacob's dream at Bethel

¹²*He had a dream in which he saw a stairway resting on the earth, with its top reaching to heaven, and the angels of God were ascending and descending on it.* ¹³*There above it stood the Lord, and He said: 'I am the Lord, the God of your father Abraham and the God of Isaac. I will give you and your descendants the land on which you are lying.* ¹⁴*Your descendants will be like the dust of the earth, and you will spread out to the west and to the east, to the north and to the south. All peoples on earth will be blessed through you and your offspring.* ¹⁵*I am with you and will watch over you wherever you go, and I will bring you back to this land. I will not leave you until I have done what I have promised you.'*

¹⁶*When Jacob awoke from his sleep, he thought, 'Surely the Lord is in this place, and I was not aware of it.'* ¹⁷*He was afraid and said, 'How awesome is this place! This is none other than the house of God; this is the gate of heaven.'*

Genesis 28:12–17

A *Jacob's dream*

There are cases of dreams giving people messages. A famous dream from the Bible is Pharaoh's dream in Genesis 41:15–32.

Pharaoh's dream

[15]Pharaoh said to Joseph, 'I had a dream, and no one can interpret it. But I have heard it said of you that when you hear a dream you can interpret it.' [16]'I cannot do it,' Joseph replied to Pharaoh, 'but God will give Pharaoh the answer he desires.' [17]Then Pharaoh said to Joseph, 'In my dream I was standing on the bank of the Nile, [18]when out of the river there came up seven cows, fat and sleek, and they grazed among the reeds. [19]After them, seven other cows came up – scrawny and very ugly and lean. I had never seen such ugly cows in all the land of Egypt. [20]The lean, ugly cows ate up the seven fat cows that came up first. [21]But even after they ate them, no one could tell that they had done so; they looked just as ugly as before. Then I woke up. [22]In my dreams I also saw seven heads of grain, full and good, growing on a single stalk. [23]After them, seven other heads sprouted – withered and thin and scorched by the east wind. [24]The thin heads of grain swallowed up the seven good heads. I told this to the magicians, but none could explain it to me.' [25]Then Joseph said to Pharaoh, 'The dreams of Pharaoh are one and the same. God has revealed to Pharaoh what he is about to do. [26]The seven good cows are seven years, and the seven good heads of grain are seven years; it is one and the same dream. [27]The seven lean, ugly cows that came up afterward are seven years, and so are the seven worthless heads of grain scorched by the east wind: They are seven years of famine. [28]It is just as I said to Pharaoh: God has shown Pharaoh what he is about to do. [29]Seven years of great abundance are coming throughout the land of Egypt, [30]but seven years of famine will follow them. Then all the abundance in Egypt will be forgotten, and the famine will ravage the land. [31]The abundance in the land will not be remembered, because the famine that follows it will be so severe. [32]The reason the dream was given to Pharaoh in two forms is that the matter has been firmly decided by God, and God will do it soon.

Genesis 41:15–32

The validity of dreams

Many people question the validity of these dreams as it is sometimes impossible to know how accurately the person is describing the dream or if the 'dreamer' is simply trying to gain attention to himself or his own ideas. As with visions, there is also the problem of trying to convey in words the actual dream so that other people might have full access to the information.

Research activity

Look for an account from another religion of a dream that is claimed to have religious significance, using the internet and/or a library. What do you think about this claim? Explain your answer.

Activities

1 Describe a recent dream you had. How well have you described the actual dream? What problems did you have with this activity? What effect did the dream have on you?

2 'God can reveal himself to people through dreams.' Do you agree? Give reasons for your answer, showing that you have thought about more than one point of view.

Extension activity

Examine what scientists claim causes people to dream. Do these explanations of dreams raise questions about dreams that give religious experiences? Explain your answer.

Summary

You should now know that dreams occur when the mind is active during sleep. Dreams can give a person new insight into the nature of God or of life. Some people claim that they get messages from God in their dreams.

3.10 Special revelation: enlightenment

Enlightenment

Enlightenment refers, in particular, to the attaining of spiritual insight that is the goal of all Buddhists. By realising that everything in this life is transitory and limited, the true Buddhist will look beyond the immediate and look for what is eternal. Once this has been achieved, the person will be free from the cycle of rebirth and reach nibbana, the state of cessation, of no interaction or involvement. While visions and dreams let the person see things in a new way, enlightenment goes beyond this to seeing the ultimate reality that lies beyond all things. All Buddhists seek to become the enlightened, to escape from the cycle of rebirth.

Objectives

Understand how enlightenment can help a believer deal with life and its pressures.

Evaluate the importance of enlightenment for believers and their faith.

Case study

The story of Siddhartha Gautama

Siddhartha Gautama lived from around 563 BCE to 483 BCE. It was at the age of 35 that he attained enlightenment. Siddhartha Gautama had tried several ways to become enlightened. One day he sat down underneath a papal (or sacred fig) tree and vowed that he would never arise until he had found the truth. The place where he sat is now called Bodh Gaya, in India. Tibetan teachings state that he meditated for 49 days, delving ever deeper into his thoughts, seeking further and further for spiritual insight. Eventually he achieved a complete and unshakeable enlightenment. From then on, Siddhartha Gautama was known as the Buddha. This term does not mean a god or a prophet, the meaning is 'one who is fully awake' or enllightened. A Buddha is a normal human being who has worked to achieve his full potential and discovered the true nature of reality.

www.psychics.co.uk/tibet/

A *Statue of the Buddha, the Enlightened One*

Guru Nanak's enlightenment

It was during his stay in Sultanpur that Nanak attained Enlightenment, at the age of thirty-six. According to popular accounts, when he and Mardana (the Muslim rabab player, his friend from his birthplace, Talwandi, who became his constant companion) went for the customary dip in the river nearby, absorbed in thoughts of God, Nanak mysteriously disappeared. Mardana raised an alarm and searched for him everywhere. His biographers state that on the third day he reappeared changed in appearance, glowing with an unusual radiance. Nanak said that he had been ushered into Divine Presence, blessed by the Almighty and told to go forth and preach the holy name of God. It was to be the mission of his life thenceforth.

The first words Nanak uttered after his enlightenment were: 'There is no Hindu, there is no Musalman'.

At a time when Hindus and Muslims were engaged in conflicts these words formed a major plank in Guru Nanak's evangelism. He spared neither group and expressed his disdain for the obsolete practices and the unthinking performance of rituals, the significance of which was lost to sight. Through this statement, he was actually pointing out that differences among various groups had overshadowed the underlying principle of all religions – that the Supreme power is one.

www.theholidayspot.com/guru_nanak_jayanti/

B   *Guru Nanak*

Enlightenment: the gaining of true knowledge, particularly in the Buddhist tradition, that frees a person from the cycle of rebirth by seeing what the truth about life really is.

Activities

1   Why is enlightenment important for some people?

2   'Believers have to accept the truth in whatever way they find it.' Do you agree? Give reasons for your answer, showing that you have thought about more than one point of view.

Kim, a 24 year old student says: 'Enlightenment enables a person to see the world for what it is: simply an illusion. If people can see beyond this illusion to the deeper reality, they will appreciate the harmony of all things. They will reach out beyond the here and now and reach the state of perfection as they are no longer bound by their worldly experiences. Enlightenment transforms everything.'

What do you think about Kim's views?

Remember that enlightenment and dreams are hard to put into words so do not spend a lot of time trying to describe them.

Summary

You should now understand that enlightenment in Buddhism is the attainment of the knowledge of the eternal reality. Enlightenment enables a person to escape from the cycle of rebirth.

3.11 | Revelation: reality and illusion

◼ Illusion

An **illusion** is something that is seen which is false or deceptive, an inaccurate interpretation of something seen or experienced. Some people think that God and religion are based on an illusion. They suggest different theories about where religion and belief in a God come from and why people claim to have religious experiences. Here are some of the theories put forward to explain why.

'God is only human qualities on a bigger scale'

Some thinkers follow the line of Ludwig Feuerbach (1804–1872) who said that God did not exist. 'God' is nothing more than the qualities humans value exaggerated to give human beings something to strive for, something to hope for. For example, humans have knowledge, God is all-knowing; humans love, God is all-loving, etc. Those who use this argument say that studying what people say about God gives them a much better insight into what is important to humans.

'God is only what society demands of people'

Some people follow the line of sociologists who say that the qualities a society tries to encourage are those which are used to describe God. Some say that leaders encourage people to think that God has set certain rules, so that the lower classes will obey those rules as part of their religion. This will make them less likely to go against the way leaders want them to live. This means that making people believe in God reinforces the hold that society has over people. For example, if the society wants people to stay in line and respect the property of the rich, they would draw up a rule that says: 'Do not steal.' Claiming that 'Do not steal' comes from God will encourage people to obey the rules more carefully.

Case study

Karl Marx

Some would follow the example of Karl Marx (1818–1883) who stated that 'religion is the opiate of the people'. What this means is that God does not exist, but if people believe in a supernatural power who will correct all that is wrong in this world and give rewards at a future point, those who are disadvantaged or suffering now will not fight to change the present order. Religion can keep order by making people accept their lowly status in society and not wish to change it.

Objectives

Examine arguments put forward that say that all religious experiences are just made up.

Assess what these alternative arguments might show about the nature of religion and of God.

Evaluate the importance of general and special revelation.

Key terms

Illusion: a false idea or belief often based on a wrong impression.

Reality: things as they truly are.

A *Karl Marx: 'Religion is the opiate of the people'*

'The future of an illusion'

The psychologist, Sigmund Freud (1856–1938), claimed that people hide behind religion to avoid having to face up to the realities of life.

Case study

Sigmund Freud

Freud claimed that God was invented by humans who wanted to avoid taking responsibility for their actions. If they could put the responsibility on God for what they did, people would not have to justify any actions. By claiming that God loves them, people would be able to live in a world that was hostile or indifferent to them without being worried. If people are afraid they cannot live happy lives. Freud claimed that people delude themselves into living happy lives by saying that God is in control and they do not have to do anything except trust in God. Freud claimed that people had to break free from any dependence on the idea of God to become fully free, fully human.

Research activity

Choose one of the thinkers mention on these pages and use the internet and/or a library to find out as much as you can about him.

Extension activity

Choose one of the theories mentioned on these ages and use the internet and/or a library to do an in-depth research about this attitude to religion.

The thinkers whose ideas have just been presented all claimed that as humans became mature and responsible for themselves, and as society got rid of its false ideas, religions and religious practices would die out.

◼ Is God a reality?

The type of explanations of God that have just been presented might seem fairly convincing at first glance, but there are questions to be asked about how valid any of these ideas are, and where the proof is.

Most religions challenge society and its values, rather than reinforce society.

The ultimate values that people have do not have to be just an extension of what they value now. It could be that the reason that they have these values is that there actually is an ultimate value that they are striving for.

Religion might help people cope with the problems of this life, but that does not prove there is no basis in fact for religion. How people use things does not reflect anything about the value or **reality** of the thing itself.

Despite what many critics of religion have said, particularly in the last 150 years, religion itself is not dying in the world. There might be a change of emphasis away from organised religion in the Western world, but there is a great focus on the spiritual side of life throughout the world. This would suggest that people sense that there is some type of absolute being, even though its existence cannot be proved.

Activities

1   Organise a debate with the resolution: 'This house believes that recent thinkers have proved that God does not exist.'

2   'Religion is simply an illusion.' Do you agree? Give reasons for your answer, showing that you have thought about more than one point of view.

Summary

You should now understand that people have different views and arguments about whether God is a reality. Since so many people follow some type of religion, this would suggest that they feel something is there.

Study tip

It is very useful if you can remember the names of the thinkers mentioned here, but it is not demanded by the specification.

3

Revelation and enlightenment – summary

For the examination you should now be able to:

✔ understand different ways in which believers claim that God can be known

✔ understand the differences between general revelation and special revelation, using examples

✔ appreciate how revelations help believers in their lives and in their beliefs

✔ explain how valid these revelations might be for the believer and for other people

✔ understand other interpretations of these revelations

✔ understand issues relating to reality and illusion.

Sample answer

1 Write an answer to the following exam question:

Explain how nature can help a person believe in God.

(6 marks)

2 Read the following sample answer.

> Believers accept that God made everything. They think that they can get a real sense of God's qualities by seeing the beauty of the world around them. Nature is full of order and harmony so this must show that God has a great sense of beauty and that He knows what people like and provides what they want. However, there is also a lot of violence and bloodshed in nature, for example, animals eating each other. Does this mean that God has a violent streak in him?

3 With a partner, discuss the sample answer. Do you think there are other things the student could have included in the answer?

4 What mark would you give this answer out of 6? Look at the mark scheme in the Introduction on page 7 (AO1). What are the reasons for the mark you have given?

Practice questions

1   Look at the picture below and answer the following questions.

(a) Explain how sacred texts are seen as special revelation.   *(3 marks)*

(b) Explain why some people would reject the idea that God reveals himself
     to believers.   *(3 marks)*

> **Study tip** Remember there are only 3 marks available for answers to these questions so focus on
> a particular area; do not try to cover all the material you have available. Use your time
> wisely.

(c) 'Revelations are only important for the individuals who get them.'
     Do you agree? Give reasons for your answer, showing that you have
     thought about more than one point of view. You must refer to religious
     arguments in your answer.   *(6 marks)*

> **Study tip** Remember that you have to present two sides of the argument, even if you are going
> to show that one side is totally wrong in your opinion: the marks come for the way you
> present your argument.

4.1 The problem of evil and the existence of God

■ Introduction

In short, **evil** can be thought of as anything that causes harm in some way, especially to people. For many people God is an all-knowing, all-powerful, all-loving being who cares for all his creatures, including human beings. Yet people suffer dreadfully, sometimes throughout their whole lives. This raises major questions in the minds of many people about God and the world.

■ An all-powerful God and the existence of evil

All-powerful (omnipotent) means that God can do all things and has power over all things. There is a lot of evil and **suffering** in the world, of many different types. God does not seem to interfere to stop all this evil and suffering. Does this mean that God has no power to stop the evil? If this is the case, then people cannot claim that God is all-powerful as evil is at least as powerful as God is.

People who have power sometimes have a great difficulty: deciding when it is best **not** to use that power. Sometimes acting to remove one problem can create many other worse problems.

Just because God does not interfere to stop evil does not prove that God does not have the power. If God always stopped evils such as war, murder or theft from happening, nothing bad could happen. This would stop anybody doing anything wrong. However, this would remove people's freedom of action or **free will**. Is this a price worth paying?

■ An all-knowing God and the existence of evil

All-knowing (omniscient) means that God knows all things. Does God know that there is evil and suffering in the world and does He know that people are dying in great pain for no real purpose? Does God know what will happen as a result of any one action? If He does not, can God be all-knowing?

Even though God might know what the outcome of any particular action will be, does that mean that He should interfere and only let good outcomes happen?

Objectives

Review the qualities of God.

Understand how the existence of evil makes these qualities difficult to assert.

Evaluate whether the evil in the world is proof that God cannot exist.

Activities

1. Think of ten examples of people (either individuals or groups) who suffer in different ways.

2. Do you think the suffering of these people can have any good side? Explain your answer.

Key terms

Evil: the opposite of good. A force or a negative power that is seen in many traditions as destructive and against God.

Suffering: the experience of something bad or painful.

Free will: having the ability to choose or determine one's own actions.

A *God being powerful means more than physical strength*

Activities

3 Give two ways that an all-powerful God could work to stop an evil event from happening. Think about what would happen to the world if God did what you suggest.

4 'God should use his power to stop all evil.' Do you agree? Give reasons for your answer, showing that you have thought about more than one point of view.

5 Think of an action you or a friend has done recently which had a bad outcome. Did you know what the outcome was likely to be before you acted? Do you think you would have acted differently if you had known what the actual outcome would be? Explain your answer.

6 'God is responsible for allowing bad things to happen.' Do you agree? Give reasons for your answer, showing that you have thought about more than one point of view.

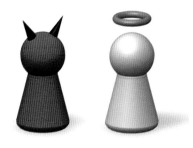

B *Is there both good and evil in the world?*

An all-loving God and the existence of evil

All-loving means that God wants what is best for his people. The fact that so many people are living and dying in great pain raises the question of whether God cares at all. If God has the power and the knowledge about these issues, surely he should do something to stop the people he loves from suffering like this. Or is God not really loving at all?

Sometimes when we love someone we have to step back and let them suffer so that they can gain something much greater. For instance, parents can give their children the freedom to go out at night in the hope that they will learn how to look after themselves and use the general guidelines that the parents have tried to instil in them as they have grown up. Children can go wild when this happens, perhaps by getting drunk or getting into fights. Would it be better for the children not to be allowed out?

Some people would argue that God is like that with humans. If he prevented humans from suffering, then he would be stopping them from developing fully, which in the long term would be even worse for them. However, people can question whether certain types of suffering, such as cancer, are needed.

Some people claim that if God is not all-powerful, all-knowing and all-loving, then there is no God. For some people, the amount of suffering in the world proves that there is no God.

Activities

7 Can you think of an event when you felt it was better for yourself or a friend to suffer, even slightly, in the short term to gain a lot more in the long term?

8 'God cannot be loving if anybody has to suffer in any way.' Do you agree? Give reasons for your answer, showing that you have thought about more than one point of view.

Discussion activity

Debate the resolution: 'There is so much suffering in the world that there cannot be a God.'

Study tip

These are difficult issues to talk about in the abstract, but much easier to deal with when you use examples.

Summary

You should now understand that the existence of evil and suffering raises issues about whether God is all-powerful, all-knowing and all-loving. However, some believe that God has a reason for allowing suffering in the world.

Introduction

Many people think that the types of suffering found in life can be divided into two groups: **natural evils** and **moral evils** (man-made evil).

Objectives

Learn what is meant by natural evil.

Understand why this form of evil raises questions about the nature of God.

Evaluate ways in which believers in a powerful and loving God explain the existence of evil and suffering.

Activity

1 a Think of as many examples of evil in the world as you can and write them in a list.

   b Go through the list of examples of evil. For each example write down if it is a natural evil, a moral evil or a combination of the two.

   c What type of evil occurs most in your list? Do you think this is a fair reflection of the true situation in life? Explain your answer.

A *A volcano erupts*

B *A country affected by drought*

Natural evil

What is natural evil?

Natural evil means the harmful effects on human beings that are caused by the way the world is structured and works.

A lot of damage is done to property and many people are hurt by what we call natural evils. Things such as earthquakes, volcanoes, tsunamis, droughts and floods cause widespread devastation. Many people say that God should have created a world in which these things did not happen, so that people would not suffer. However, there might be another way of looking at this problem.

Key terms

Natural evil: the harm or damage that is done to people and creation as a result of the forces of nature and the structure of the Earth.

Moral evil: the harm that results from a bad choice made by human beings misusing their free will.

What causes natural evil?

Let's think about earthquakes, volcanoes and tsunamis as examples. What causes them? The earth has a molten metal core and the crust of the earth is made up of plates that come into close contact with each other, sometimes overlapping slightly.

- **Earthquakes**: the earth spins round on its axis and revolves around the sun. This motion of the world causes movement throughout the planet. The tectonic plates move and when they rub against each other it can cause an earthquake.

- **Volcanoes**: the spinning of the earth causes pressure to build up in the core. This pressure is released through vents and openings in the form of volcanoes. The vast majority of the volcanoes are under the sea where they do not cause any harm.

- **Tsunamis**: a tsunami is caused when two tectonic plates rub against each other under water causing a movement of the water that results in a massive tidal wave when the water comes into contact with land.

Why does natural evil hurt people?

All these events happen because of the way the world is structured. The fact that people are hurt by these events is unfortunate, but can God always be blamed for this? People choose to live near volcanoes because the land is good for growing crops, although they know that there is a chance that the volcano will erupt. Is it really fair to blame God when those people are hurt?

It might be possible to say that God should have made the earth without any faults, but would it be the earth if it did not spin around, creating gravity and the day and night?

Most of the natural evils people complain about only happen because the earth is the way it is. If earth had been designed differently, it might not have allowed humans to evolve. What would be better: to have an earth with the current problems or to have a different earth that did not contain free human beings?

Activity

2 Consider the following questions:

a Do people complain when there is a volcano underwater? Why not?

b Why are people hurt when a volcano erupts on land? Whose fault is it when people are hurt by the volcanic eruption? Why were people there to be hurt?

c What causes tectonic plate movement? What would happen if the earth did not spin around or revolve around the sun?

d 'God made the earth the way it is to allow humans to live their lives as they do.' Do you think this was the right thing for God to do? Explain your answer.

Summary

You should now know that evil can be divided into two basic types: natural evil which is the result of how the earth is and how it works; man-made (moral) evil when people freely choose to hurt each other. The existence of evil and suffering in the world raises questions about belief in God.

◼ Moral (man-made) evil

What is moral evil?

A lot of pain and suffering in the world is caused by humans ill-treating each other, sometimes referred to as 'man's inhumanity to man'. All of this type of suffering is the result of deliberate actions by one person trying to get his/her own way, regardless of the hurt it causes to other people, and even sometimes to themselves. Theft, murder, war, aggressive behaviour, bullying, racism, exploitation of the poor, slavery, concentration camps … the list is almost endless.

What causes moral evil?

Humans choose to take the actions they do and so must be held responsible for their behaviour. Guns do not fire themselves. A knife can be used for good things (such as a scalpel in a surgeon's hand used to save a person's life) or for evil things (such as stabbing someone). It is not the instrument itself that is good or bad, but simply the way it is used or, rather, the intention for which it is used. Most actions could be for a good purpose or a bad purpose (for example, a camera can be used to take a happy family portrait or to take pornographic pictures). It is the intentions that ultimately decide whether an action is good or bad. Most people believe that God has given the human race free will and it is up to humans how they use this free will.

A   *Skulls from the killing fields of Cambodia*

Auschwitz, a prisoner camp in World War Two

Prisoners received three meals per day. In the morning, they received only half a litre of 'coffee', or rather boiled water with a grain-based coffee substitute added, or 'tea' – a herbal brew. These beverages were usually unsweetened. The noon meal consisted of about a litre of soup, the main ingredients of which were potatoes, rutabaga, and small amounts of groats, rye flour, and Avo food extract. The soup was unappetizing, and newly arrived prisoners were often unable to eat it, or could do so only in disgust. Supper consisted of about 300 grams of black bread, served with about 25 grams of sausage, or margarine, or a tablespoon of marmalade or cheese. The bread served in the evening was supposed to cover the needs of the following morning as well, although the famished prisoners usually consumed the whole portion at once. The low nutritional value of these meals should be noted.

The combination of insufficient nutrition with hard labour contributed to the destruction of the organism, which gradually used up its stores of fat, muscle mass, and the tissues of the internal organs. This led to emaciation and starvation sickness; the cause of a significant number of deaths in the camp. A prisoner suffering from starvation sickness could easily fall victim to selection for the gas chambers.

B *Auschwitz camp today*

Contributed by Jacek Lachendro

Activities

1 Choose three examples of 'man's inhumanity to man.' Explain:
   a What caused these examples?
   b How much suffering did each lead to (think beyond the immediate victims)?
   c What do these examples show about people?

2 Choose two examples of when a particular item could be used to cause damage or to make good happen. Explain fully what makes the actions good or bad.

3 'God cannot be held responsible when people choose to misuse his creation.' Do you agree? Give reasons for your answer, showing that you have thought about more than one point of view.

Research activity

Draw up a list of twenty different examples of moral evil. How easy was this to do? What might this suggest about moral evil?

Extension activity

Read the novel *The Boy in the Striped Pyjamas* by John Boyre.

Summary

You should now understand that the human race has free will to do good or bad and moral evil causes suffering. This raises questions about the nature of God.

Study tip

Be careful that you do not just give examples of moral evils. Show how these evils raise questions about the nature of God.

Most religions have some explanation of how evil began (or the origin of evil), often described in the form of a story. Very few people would read these stories as historically factual accounts of the origin of evil, but the stories often contain an underlying universal truth which many people can understand and accept. As examples, two accounts are presented in this book: the Judaeo-Christian story of Adam and Eve and the Islamic story of Iblis. There are many others.

■ Adam and Eve

The Fall of Man

[1]Now the serpent was more crafty than any of the wild animals the LORD God had made. He said to the woman, 'Did God really say, "You must not eat from any tree in the garden"?' [2]The woman said to the serpent, 'We may eat fruit from the trees in the garden, [3]but God did say, "You must not eat fruit from the tree that is in the middle of the garden, and you must not touch it, or you will die." ' [4]"You will not surely die,' the serpent said to the woman. [5]'For God knows that when you eat of it your eyes will be opened, and you will be like God, knowing good and evil.' [6]When the woman saw that the fruit of the tree was good for food and pleasing to the eye, and also desirable for gaining wisdom, she took some and ate it. She also gave some to her husband, who was with her, and he ate it. [7]Then the eyes of both of them were opened, and they realized they were naked; so they sewed fig leaves together and made coverings for themselves. [8]Then the man and his wife heard the sound of the LORD God as he was walking in the garden in the cool of the day, and they hid from the LORD God among the trees of the garden. [9]But the LORD God called to the man, 'Where are you?' [10]He answered, 'I heard you in the garden, and I was afraid because I was naked; so I hid.' [11]And he said, 'Who told you that you were naked? Have you eaten from the tree that I commanded you not to eat from?' [12]The man said, 'The woman you put here with me—she gave me some fruit from the tree, and I ate it.' [13]Then the LORD God said to the woman, 'What is this you have done?' The woman said, 'The serpent deceived me, and I ate.' [14]So the LORD God said to the serpent, 'Because you have done this, cursed are you above all the livestock and all the wild animals! You will crawl on your belly and you will eat dust all the days of your life. [15]And I will put enmity between you and the woman, and between your offspring and hers; he will crush your head, and you will strike his heel.' [16]To the woman he said, 'I will greatly increase your pains in childbearing; with pain you will give birth to children. Your desire will be for your husband, and he will rule over you.' [17]To Adam he said, 'Because you listened to your wife and ate from the tree about which I commanded you, "You must not eat of it," 'Cursed is the ground because of you; through painful toil you will eat of it all the days

A Eve was tempted by the serpent

Objectives

Examine the story of Adam and Eve from the Bible.

Understand the message of this story about the role of God in the creation of evil.

Evaluate the importance of this story about the origins of evil.

Activities

1. Why does God tell Adam and Eve not to eat from the tree? Do you think this is fair? Explain your answer.

2. Why does the serpent ask, 'Did God really say, "You must not eat from any tree in the garden"?'? What is he trying to get Eve to focus on?

3. Why does Eve give some of the fruit to Adam? Is this right? Explain your answer.

4. Why do Adam and Eve hide from God? What does this show about the effects of sin?

5. Why does Adam blame Eve? Is he right to do this? Explain your answer.

6. Does God punish Adam and Eve? Explain your answer.

7. 'If God had not made the serpent, evil would not be in the world; so evil is God's fault.' Do you agree? Give reasons for your answer, showing that you have thought about more than one point of view.

of your life. [18]It will produce thorns and thistles for you, and you will eat the plants of the field. [19]By the sweat of your brow you will eat your food until you return to the ground, since from it you were taken; for dust you are and to dust you will return.' [20]Adam named his wife Eve, because she would become the mother of all the living. [21]The LORD God made garments of skin for Adam and his wife and clothed them. [22]And the LORD God said, 'The man has now become like one of us, knowing good and evil. He must not be allowed to reach out his hand and take also from the tree of life and eat, and live forever.' [23]So the LORD God banished him from the Garden of Eden to work the ground from which he had been taken. [24]After he drove the man out, he placed on the east side of the Garden of Eden cherubim and a flaming sword flashing back and forth to guard the way to the tree of life.

Genesis 3:1-24

B   *God sends Adam and Eve out of the garden*

On a first reading, this story might seem very simple: the serpent tempted Adam and Eve and they gave in. In this way evil entered into the world.

However, there is much more to the story than that. This story is not about something that happens in the past but something that is happening every day. God provided everything that humans need to be happy and he gives them one very special gift: the gift of freedom,. not to eat of one particular tree. This is not a great demand but it does mean that Adam and Eve have a choice. The serpent stresses what Adam and Eve are not allowed to do. No one likes to be told what to do so Adam and Eve assert their independence from God. God allows Adam and Eve to acknowledge what they have done. Then he lets them live with the consequences of their decision: they cannot expect God to provide everything they want. They now have to look after themselves and they will find it difficult.

Interpretations of this story

On a first reading, this story might seem very simple: the serpent tempted Adam and Eve and they gave in. In this way evil entered into the world.

However, there is much more to the story than that. Adam means 'man' (as in mankind) and this story is not about something that happened in the past, but something that is happening every day. In the story, God provides everything that humans need to be happy and he gives them one very special gift: the gift of free will. This is shown by his request for Adam and Eve not to eat the fruit of one particular tree. This is not a great demand, but it does mean that Adam and Eve have a choice: they are not just God's puppets, always doing what he wants. The serpent phrases his question in such a way that it stresses what Adam and Eve are not allowed to do. No one likes to be told what they must not do, so Adam and Eve assert their independence from God by doing what they want, rather than what God has asked.

God allows Adam and Eve to acknowledge what they have done. Then he lets them live with the consequences of their decision: they want to be independent of God, so they cannot expect God to provide everything they want. They now have to look after themselves and they will find it difficult. By giving them clothes before throwing them out of the garden, God shows that he still cares for Adam and Eve.

links

To read the Islamic story of Iblis, see page 88.

To read the Islamic story of Iblis, see page 88.

Activities

8   Either write a poem or draw a strip cartoon to give the message of the Fall of Adam and Eve.

9   'Humans are to blame for the presence of evil in the world.' Do you agree? Give reasons for your answer, showing that you have thought about more than one point of view.

Study tip

There is not a specific story about the origin of evil that you will be tested on, but you need to be able to talk about one story in the exam.

Summary

You should now know that The main focus of the story in Genesis 3 is that God gave humans free will. They misused this and brought evil into the world because they have to live with the consequences of their choice.

4.5 The origins of evil: Iblis

■ Iblis

Another story about how evil began can be found in the Qur'an. This is the story of Iblis.

Objectives

Examine the story of Iblis from the Qur'an.

Understand the message of this story about the role of God in the creation of evil.

Evaluate the importance of this story about the origins of evil.

Activities

1. Read the story of Iblis and put it in your own words.
2. Explain the major differences between the Qur'an story of Iblis, Adam and Eve and the Genesis story of the Fall.

Beliefs and teachings

Almighty Allâh also revealed: And surely, We created you (your father Adam) and then gave you shape (the noble shape of a human being), then We told the angels, 'Prostrate to Adam', and they prostrated, except Iblis, he refused to be among those who prostrate.

Allâh said: 'What prevented you (O Iblis) that you did not prostrate when I commanded you?'

Iblis said: 'I am better than him (Adam), You created me from fire and him You created from clay.'

Allâh said: 'O Iblis get down from this (Paradise), it is not for you to be arrogant here. Get out for you are of those humiliated and disgraced.'

Iblis said: 'Allow me respite till the Day they are raised up (Day of Resurrection).'

Allâh said: 'You are of those allowed respite.'

Iblis said: 'Because You have sent me astray, surely I will sit in wait against them (human beings) on Your Straight Path. Then I will come to them from before them and behind them, from their right and from their left and You will not find most of them as thankful ones (they will not be dutiful to You).'

Allâh said: 'Get out from Paradise, disgraced and expelled. Whoever of them (mankind) will follow you, then surely I will fill Hell with you all.'

'And O Adam! Dwell you and your wife in Paradise, and eat thereof as you both wish, but approach not this tree otherwise you both will be of the Zaleemeen (unjust and wrongdoers).'

Then Satan whispered suggestions to them both in order to uncover that which was hidden from them of their private parts before, he said: 'Your Lord did not forbid you this tree save you should become angels or become of the immortals.'

Satan swore by Allâh to them both saying: 'Verily I am one of the sincere well wishers for you both.' So he misled them with deception. Then when they tasted of the tree, that which was hidden from them of their shame (private parts) became manifest to them and they began to stick together the leaves of Paradise over themselves (in order to cover their shame).

Their Lord called out to them saying 'Did I not forbid you that tree and tell you, Verily Satan is an open enemy unto you?'

They said: 'Our Lord! We have wronged ourselves. If You forgive us not, and bestow not upon us Your Mercy, we shall certainly be of the losers.'

Allâh said: 'Get down one of you an enemy to the other (that is, Adam, Eve, and Satan, etc). On earth will be a dwelling place for you and an enjoyment, for a time.' He said: 'therein you shall live, and therein you shall die, and from it you shall be brought out (resurrected).'

Qur'an 7:11–25

In the Qur'an, the angel Iblis refused to bow down before mankind as Allah wished and so Iblis was sent from heaven. Iblis now travels around the world getting people to reject Allah and to join Iblis in hell. Adam and Eve are led astray by Satan (Iblis). Adam and Eve turn to the Merciful Allah in sorrow and ask forgiveness.

Research activity

Find an account or an explanation of the presence of evil from another religious tradition. Or find an alternative version from Judaism, Christianity or Islam.

Activities

3 According to the Qur'an, who is to blame for evil in the world? Explain your answer.

4 'The story of Iblis explains the presence of evil in the world better than the Genesis story of Adam and Eve.' Do you agree? Give reasons for your answer, showing that you have thought about more than one point of view.

A   *An artist's impression of Iblis*

While there are many different stories about the origin of evil in the world, very few of these stories put the blame on God. The major religions see God as the creator of all that is good (see Chapter 5). Evil is often viewed as a distortion away from what God wanted, usually connected with the misuse of free will. The main message is that God allows evil, he does not will it.

Extension activity

Compare two different accounts of the presence of evil. Comment on both the similarities and the differences in the stories and their messages. Which do you prefer (if either) and why?

Summary

You should now know that different religions explain the origin of evil in different ways, but few religions blame God directly for evil. In the Qur'an, Iblis rejects Allah and goes about persuading others also to reject Allah.

4.6 The existence of evil and suffering (1)

■ Arguments for the need for evil

Humans need a contrast

Look at these two interesting images.

Objectives

Review the arguments put forward by some people who think that evil has a positive role in life.

Assess these arguments in the light of the amount of suffering there is in the world.

Evaluate whether a lesser amount of suffering might produce the same results.

Activities

1. Which of the two images (**A** or **B**) do you prefer? Why?
2. Would it be right to call these pictures? Explain your answer.

A *Do you like this image? Why or why not?*

B *Do you like this image? Why or why not?*

As with these pictures, many people think that we need bad to show us what is meant by good. If everything was the same, we would have no understanding of anything. For example, if everything in the world was red, then we would not be able to differentiate things. We would have no sense of what is blue, green, and so on. We would not even be able to appreciate the red, as we would not have anything to compare it to.

If everything in the world was good, people would have no knowledge of anything bad. If nothing ever went wrong, then life would have no meaning since people would not be able to understand what good and bad meant. Good and bad would not exist in people's minds. Everything would appear to be of the same value. If this was the case, nothing that I did and nothing that I liked would have any importance. It would be impossible to value one thing over another, as there would be nothing to judge anything against.

Activities

3 Could you value good if there was no bad? Explain your answer.

4 'People do not need the amount of suffering there is in the world to have an understanding of what good is.' Do you agree? Give reasons for your answer, showing that you have thought about more than one point of view.

Study tip

To help make sense of this idea, imagine what life would be like if everybody always gained full marks in tests, no matter how much effort they made.

Evil is necessary to allow people to know what is good and also to be able to choose what is good. According to some thinkers, people need evil to show us what is good. In this way we can appreciate both the good and the bad, but we do need them both in order to appreciate the other one.

God only created the good

According to most creation stories, all that God made was good. God could not make anything bad as evil is not part of God's nature. However, God gave humans free will and, as shown in the story of Adam and Eve, they used this freedom to do what they wanted, not what God wanted. Evil does not exist in itself, it is only a lack of good. God wants the world to be perfect, but the world has been ruined by things failing to reach the standard that God wants. According to some traditions, it was the choice of Adam and Eve that brought evil into the world. It was the fault of human beings, not God, that made the whole of creation fall into imperfection. This was against the will of God, but he accepted it as a necessary element of people being free to make decisions. As St Augustine said, 'All evil is either sin or the effects of sin.'

Activity

5 'Humans must take the blame for the amount of evil in the world.' Do you agree? Give reasons for your answer, showing that you have thought about more than one point of view.

Extension activity

Write a story about a world in which nothing bad is possible. How easy is this task? Explain your answer.

Summary

You should now understand that people cannot appreciate what is good in life without having the contrast with evil. Believers often state that God only made good things; evil is a lack of good.

The world as a place of preparation

Experience and learning

Life is about developing. People are growing, experiencing things and learning all the time. For this to happen effectively, people need to be able to experience good and bad things. If a footballer scored a goal each time he touched the ball, there would be no challenge for him and, equally, he would never try to improve his technique. The older people become, the more they can develop. Many people believe that this life is only a preparation for the next life. People need to learn now in order to make better choices in the future.

Activities

1. In pairs, list five things that you have learned to do by experiencing them. Think of the last five years of your life. What are you allowed to do now that you would not have been allowed to do five years ago? Do you think this is right?

2. 'Children should be allowed to try anything at any age.' Do you agree? Give reasons for your answer, showing that you have thought about more than one point of view.

People can only really learn by making mistakes themselves and by seeing the mistakes others make too. Perhaps this is not a bad thing. Without challenges people would not be able to develop mentally or emotionally.

Research activity

Use the internet and/or a library to find five slogans or mottos from different groups, organisations or clubs that stress the need for striving to be the best. Examples could include Everton Football Club, The Royal Air Force etc.

A *We learn by experience*

Activities

3. Imagine that your parents had decided when you were six months old that they did not want any evil coming to you and so they locked you in a padded room where you could not injure yourself. They provided for all your physical needs and made sure that you never came into contact with anybody that could cause you harm or pain in any way. Would your parents have done you a favour? Explain your answer.

4. Think of people you know who are given everything they want by their parents. What type of people do they tend to be? Why?

Study tip

Look back on your own life and think of a really difficult thing you had to do or accept. How much difference has that made to your life?

We learn as we experience and without experiencing we cannot learn. If everything in our lives went well, without any upset, harm or disappointment, we could never become mature and responsible people. If we cannot learn to make choices and to live with the results of our choices, life is meaningless. For us to be able to make choices, there has to be good as well as bad in life. It has to be possible for things to go wrong. We need the possibility of evil to enable us to grow as mature people. This is sometimes called '**soul-making**' and this life is called a 'vale of soul-making'.

'Soul-making' means that people's characters are able to develop and become stronger as they react to different types of experience. Athletes have to push themselves hard to develop their skills and strength. However, this is only part of their training. The ability to get out at all hours of the day and in all types of weather, a willingness not to go out with friends to a party before a race, and so on, all affect their personality and make them stronger in ways that go beyond athletic ability. In the same way, people who have to struggle with the demands of life end up as more complete human beings. Life has helped them to develop their personalities fully. The hardships and negative experiences in life are all a part of this development and without them people would be stunted as human beings. There is a famous saying of 'no pain, no gain' and this reflects the same idea: if you can struggle with the demands of life, you may end up a far stronger person.

Religious thoughts on this life as a preparation

For Christians, this life is a preparation for the afterlife in heaven. The happiness of heaven has to be accepted. People who are not able to make real choices will never be able to appreciate what God offers them in the afterlife.

Most other religions have similar ideas about the relationship of this life to the afterlife, though some see the afterlife as a rebirth or reincarnation on this earth. But equally for these believers, the choices that people make in this life are important, as they determine the nature of the next life.

However, there are also many people who feel that individual development cannot justify the amount of suffering in this life, particularly the suffering of innocent people, such as millions of children starving to death.

Key terms
Soul-making: the belief that suffering makes it possible for people to 'grow' into more mature individuals.

Extension activity
Write a story about a world where people did not have to make any effort to achieve things. What type of world would this be? Would you want to live there? Explain your answer.

⊙⊙links

Religious beliefs about the afterlife are covered in more detail in Chapter 6.

Activities

5 In your own words, explain why some say that evil is needed for people to make decisions.

6 'Everyone should suffer in their lives.' Do you agree? Give reasons for your answer, showing that you have thought about more than one point of view.

Summary

You should now understand that people learn by experience and by making mistakes. They have to live in a world where things go wrong. Religions teach that what happens after death is affected by the choices believers make in this life, so these choices must be free.

4.8 The free will defence

The free will defence

The **free will defence** is based on a specific understanding of what it means to be human. Humans have the ability to make choices that affect themselves and other people. Humans are conscious of their choices.

Free will and God

If God wants people to respond to his love, people must be totally free to love or to reject that love. This means that God cannot interfere with the choices people make, no matter how much he is hurt by the damage people do to themselves and to each other. Any form of interference by God is stopping humans from being free. For free choices to be made, people have to live in a world where things can, and do, go wrong.

God cannot interfere when people decide to go to war. If two aircraft are on a collision course, God cannot interfere and make them suddenly miles apart because if he did it on one occasion he would have to do it on every occasion. This would mean God taking over the running of people's lives. If God has allowed life to evolve, then he cannot suddenly interfere when some particular mutation, such as cancer, is undesirable. God must either allow things to follow their own course or he has to deliberately guide them in the way he wants them to go, thus removing human freedom. The same type of approach would apply to situations such as famine that are often the result of bad choices made by humans as well as adverse weather conditions. God might not be directly controlling these things. This is not because God does not have the power to do so, but because if he used this power on these occasions, then he would be interfering with people's freedom.

A *Should a loving God interfere in human decisions?*

Activities

4 Can an animal show love or are its reactions to humans based on what it can get from them (for example, food)?

5 Can a person ever buy love? Explain your answer.

6 Can a person ever be forced to love another person? Explain your answer.

7 What do these examples show about the nature of love?

8 Should God interfere in these situations?

a Two airplanes carrying more than 300 people are on a collision course.

b A famous doctor who is on the brink of producing a cure for all forms of cancer is stabbed by a mugger in the street and is dying.

c Four million young children are facing slow starvation in Africa because they have no food.

9 'If God starts to interfere in any way he destroys the freedom that all people need.' Do you agree? Give reasons for your answer, showing that you have thought about more than one point of view.

Study tip

To help with this topic, just think about yourself: do you like people telling you what to do or limiting your choices? Why not?

B *The freedom to choose*

Case study

Beth is a 66 year old widow. She says: 'When my husband Bill was dying a slow painful death of cancer, I blamed God and said that he had no right to do this to us. If God was loving why should Bill suffer like that. But Bill reminded me of all the good times that we had shared together, of all the decisions that we had made together and individually. Sometimes things went our way and other times went against us. Yet there always seemed to be something positive to gain from every event. We learned to be happy through our choices. That made our life together good. I don't like it when things go bad, but I would rather they went bad than we never had any choice.'

What do you think of Beth's views?

Free will and natural evil

The free will defence not only covers the need for people to be able to do anything they want, no matter how many other people are hurt by their actions, it also allows for natural evils.

If people lived in a world where unexpected disasters did not happen, if everything was predictable, then there would be no opportunity for people to take responsibility for their actions. Freedom not only means being able to choose, but also being able to accept the consequences. If we could absolutely guarantee that a particular action would have a very specific result, then there would be no real freedom, no real choice. The reason millions of pounds are spent on the National Lottery each year is because people do not know that they are going to lose.

Life is full of these types of examples; it is the unexpected that makes people aware of their freedom. If natural disasters did not happen, life would be very predictable. If there was a major hurricane on 5 October every year, people might not like it, but they could do something that ensured they were not harmed by the hurricane. However, this kind of predictability removes all value from life. For the unexpected to happen, there has to be the chance of total disaster happening as well as total triumph.

Activity

10 'God should allow people enough freedom to enjoy life, but not so much that they suffer badly.' Do you agree? Give reasons for your answer, showing that you have thought about more than one point of view.

Summary

You should now know and understand the belief that God creates out of love so he must respect the free will of the people he creates to accept or reject that love. This argument is called the free will defence. For freedom to be exercised we must have a world where things can and do go wrong.

4.9 The concept of karma and the existence of evil

The concept of karma

Karma is an important idea or belief in the Eastern religions, notably Buddhism, Hinduism and Sikhism, though there are some differences between them in their understanding of karma. It is not found in the religions of Judaism, Christianity and Islam.

Karma is basically the law of consequences. It plays a large part in the beliefs about the cycle of reincarnation and rebirth. Every action is seen to produce either good or bad results (or consequences) for the person who performs the action. These consequences will come into play at some stage, maybe at a later point in this life or possibly in the next reincarnation. Good actions have good consequences and build up good karma, bad actions have evil consequences. For instance, if you live a good life, taking care of other people, this will lead to a positive result in the next life. This could be either as a reward, or it might be that your soul has developed qualities that make the next existence better for you. Equally, if you have been selfish, cowardly or cruel in this life, your next life will be affected negatively.

According to many believers, if you are suffering in this life, it is because you have built up bad karma from previous lifetimes. Karma is not seen as reward and punishment, but the inevitable consequences of actions.

Activities

1 Explain the idea of karma in your own words.

2 'A person who is suffering in this life deserves what happens to them.' Do you agree? Give reasons for your answer, showing that you have thought about more than one point of view.

Karma and evil

Karma (kamma) is affected by the build-up of the good and bad things people do. For this to happen, there has to be the possibility of bad actions. If people could only do good actions, then their actions could not really be called good and, therefore, they should not be rewarded for their actions. Suffering is the consequence of bad actions. Evil brings about suffering and this helps to show a contrast between good and bad actions.

- **In Hinduism**, the challenge for everybody is to escape the cycle of reincarnation. They do this by achieving moksha, liberation, when no more karma is built up and the person is no longer reborn when they die. Suffering and evil are no longer relevant for them.

- **For Sikhs**, karma is the law that brings back the results of actions to the person doing them; so a good action leads to some kind of reward, while a bad action leads to suffering.

- **In Buddhism**, karma is connected to the world of suffering which affects every life. The faithful Buddhist tries to live a life free from desire, hate and delusion, to reach true enlightenment. In this way karma is left behind.

A *Hindus aim to escape the cycle of reincarnation*

Beliefs and teachings

Sikhism

The following are quotes from the Guru Granth Sahib that show the effect of karma:

'By the karma of past actions, the robe of this physical body is obtained. By the grace, the gate of liberation is found.'

'The body is the field of karma in this age; whatever you plant, you shall harvest.'

'Born because of the karma of their past mistakes, they make more mistakes, and fall into mistakes.'

'Those who have the blessing of good karma, meet with the Lord.'

Beliefs and teachings

Hinduism

'A person who performs good Karma (deeds) is always held in high esteem.'

'A person can achieve everything by being simple and humble.'

from the Rig Veda

'Work done with selfish motives is inferior by far to the selfless service or Karma-yoga.'

from the Bhagavad Gita

Beliefs and teachings

Buddhism

'Countless rebirths lie ahead, both good and bad. The effects of karma (actions) are inevitable, and in previous lifetimes we have accumulated negative karma which will inevitably have its fruition in this or future lives. Just as someone witnessed by police in a criminal act will eventually be caught and punished, so we too must face the consequences of faulty actions we have committed in the past, there is no way to be at ease; those actions are irreversible; we must eventually undergo their effects.'

His Holiness the Dalai Lama, from Kindness, Clarity and Insight

For many believers in these religions, the current suffering is only a part of a whole experience that has to include every rebirth or reincarnation that the individual will go through. Some people would argue that by the time people have lived through many reincarnations they have experienced all the good and all the bad things that life has to offer them. If this is true, by the time the escape from rebirth or reincarnation has been achieved, each individual has had the same total experience of life as everybody else.

Extension activity

Use the internet and/or a library to find two other quotes about reincarnation or rebirth. Explain the quotes in your own words.

Activities

3   Why is karma important in the cycle of rebirth and reincarnation?

4   'Karma makes good sense of the problem of evil and suffering.' Do you agree? Give reasons for your answer, showing that you have thought about more than one point of view.

Summary

You should now know and understand that karma is the law of consequences in which good actions build up good karma and bad actions build up bad karma. The consequences of good and bad karma can take place either in this life or in the next reincarnation/rebirth. Once a person has escaped reincarnation/rebirth, karma comes to an end.

Study tip

You will not be expected to know the differences between the Buddhist, Hindu and Sikh ideas of karma. A general understanding of the basic idea of karma will be enough for the exam.

How believers respond to situations of evil and suffering

In all the major religions the faithful are called to help people in need. Nearly all believers who accept that God is personal and caring find it difficult to ignore the sufferings of anybody. This is because they feel that God does not want to see his creatures suffer in any way; emotionally or physically. However, they also accept that suffering and evil have a role to play in life and suffering cannot be removed totally while the earth exists. No individual can remove all the effects of suffering and evil by himself, but this does not give the believer an excuse for not trying to make some difference to the lives of those who are in need, even if this effort is inadequate. They feel that doing something is much better than doing nothing.

There are many examples in all walks of life of people making a difference:

- an individual setting out to make life better for the outcasts of society, for example, Mother Theresa of Calcutta
- trying to get rid of oppressive rules, as the Buddhist monks are trying to do in Tibet
- removing social inequalities, as Mahatma Gandhi did in India
- fighting against racial discrimination, as Nelson Mandela did in South Africa
- helping the victims of famine and disasters, as the volunteers of Muslim Aid do
- trying to improve the lot of the homeless and drug addicts, as the members of the Salvation Army do
- caring for the needy in the locality of the gurdwara, as Sikhs do.

Objectives

Know how believers respond in practice to situations of evil and suffering.

Understand what the believers' responses show about their attitude to evil and suffering.

Study tip

In some ways it is easiest to start this topic by looking at what people do and what their motives are in the fight against evil and its effects.

Research activity

Use the internet and/or a library to find an individual, group or organisation that is working to remove the effects of some type of evil in the world. Investigate what they do and how successful they are.

A *A woman begging on the street*

The list is endless, but it reflects people's basic attitude that they have a duty to try to bring about positive changes in the world. Many believers would agree with the saying that 'for evil to conquer good, people only have to do nothing.' They are not prepared to let evil situations win and they are not prepared to leave it to other people to do something. Respect for fellow human beings and a belief in their equal value makes them want to act to help those who are suffering.

There are so many signs of evil in the world that people could easily get discouraged and give up hope of things ever getting better. Religions teach that all people have value and that it is the duty of everyone to ensure that this value is respected. Many teach that God wants what is best for his people and God needs people to cooperate to bring this about. Some people respond to the sufferings of others because it is one way to either build up their own karma or to gain a reward in heaven. Most believers simply respond because they want to change things, not for any selfish motives.

Extension activity

Use the internet and/or a library to research and compare the efforts of three different types of organisations to get rid of evil. How successful have they been? Are the situations they are addressing getting better or worse? Do you think their efforts are worthwhile no matter what the outcome? Explain your answer.

Case study

Ahmed is a 28 year old Muslim from Britain who has done voluntary work for Muslim Aid. He has spent three years helping drought victims in Africa. He says: 'When I arrived at the village, everyone was in a really bad way. The little water that they had left was dirty and unhygienic. People had little hope but a lot of determination to try to get beyond the problem. What they needed most was some guidance and support but also some equipment that they could not afford. Muslim Aid provided the equipment that allowed us to dig a deep well until we hit the water table. The villagers then followed our advice and example in reinforcing the walls of the well to ensure it didn't get blocked. Once the water was available, there was a new feeling of hope and a new confidence that they could face the other problems. Life is still very hard, and only a small part of the village life has changed, but with people working together, one evil at least has been overcome.'

Activities

1   Draw up a list of ten individuals or groups who are trying to make things better for those in need. How successful are their efforts in the long term? Do you think it is worth their while doing what they are doing? Explain your answer.

2   Why will evil conquer if good people do nothing?

3   Try asking a person why they gave a contribution to someone in need, for example, buying the *Big Issue*. Most people will only give a vague, often dismissive, answer. Why do you think this is? Is it, perhaps, because most people do not actually think when they respond to people in need, they just feel it is important to help? Does this matter? Explain your answer.

4   Does a person's reasons for giving help to those in need really matter as long as the help is given? Explain your answer.

B   *The Jubilee Debt Campaign – an example of a positive response to human suffering*

Summary

You should now know about believers feel that it is their duty to help those in need, as it is showing God's love for all people. Their respect for human beings and a desire to ensure that good conquers evil makes them want to act.

4.11 Do people need evil and suffering?

Arguments for the need for evil and suffering

A few people might argue that if there were no evil or suffering in the world, people would not be able to help out those in need. This would mean that people would become very shallow and selfish. When people are hurting, others are very quick to come to their help. However, consider the following:

- Does this mean that people are usually selfish and that it is only when they are face-to-face with human tragedy that people can be bothered to help?
- Do people do this because they feel guilty that they are well-off while others are suffering?
- Does suffering bring home to the comfortably-off how lucky they really are? For example, do the people in wealthy Northern countries need to see disasters in Africa to make them realise just how well-off they are themselves?

People in Britain are among the 20 per cent of the world's population that use up 80 per cent of the world's resources, but many people do not realise or believe this. If there were no reports of major disasters on the television and in the papers, most people would not even think about those who are less well-off. However, just because no one reports suffering does not mean that people are not always in need. When evil and suffering are reported, people do respond, usually very positively.

The way people respond also reflects a lot of what is inside them as individuals. There are some people who will not help, who seem happy to see others suffer. They may believe that their present situation is hard enough and they cannot think about that of others; they may be very unhappy and unable to consider others; they may not value their life very much and therefore be unable to respond positively to the suffering of others.

Religious responses to the need for evil and suffering

Most religions stress the value and dignity of every person as a creature of God.

- Buddhists see suffering as a part of life, but a part that has to be dealt with and not ignored.
- Christianity stresses the importance of humanity by claiming that God took on the limitations of the human condition, that Jesus went through all the pains and suffering of life as a proof that God loves each person. There is nothing that can happen to a human being that God is unaware of. This does not mean that suffering and pain are acceptable to God, but that they are understood by God and that humans are helped to deal with them in the love of God.
- The Muslim stress on the need for zakat (alms-giving) to help those in need is another example of how religions try to deal with the effects of suffering.

Objectives

Understand why people see a value in suffering.

Evaluate whether evil and suffering make a positive difference in the world.

Study tip

Start this section by looking at what difference it would make if believers ignored other people who suffered.

Extension activity

Examine the answers to the problem of evil provided by two different religions. Bring out what areas they have in common about the way believers think and respond to evil and evil situations. Also show how the two religions take a different stance on certain areas of the problem. What is your personal response to the position taken by each of these religions? Explain your answer.

Research activities

1   Research a situation where believers are helping those in need. Examples include the work of the Salvation Army, the work of Islamic Aid to help the starving, etc.

2   'People need other people to suffer so that they can fulfil their religious duties.' Do you agree? Give reasons for your answer, showing that you have thought about more than one point of view.

A   *Slum in a less economically developed country*

The value that comes from a religious belief may help people to see suffering and evil as a somewhat necessary element in life, even though evil is not a positive thing in itself.

Religious people try hard to find a solution for the problem of evil and some of the proposed solutions have been considered. However, the majority of believers are unhappy with most of these possible solutions. Some people take the line, with Job in the Old Testament (a part of the Bible used by Jews and Christians), that all they can do is ask the questions and feel frustrated when the answers cannot be found. Believers do not want to blame God for the existence of evil and they do not feel that evil and suffering are a part of God's plan for human beings. However, other solutions escape them. All that is left for them is to do everything in their power to reduce the effects of evil, in the hope that, one day, evil and suffering will come to an end.

Discussion activity

As a class, debate the topic: 'Evil and suffering make life worthwhile.'

Summary

You should now understand why some religious believers argue that evil and suffering are necessary and that some good may come from suffering. Many others do not claim to understand why there is evil and suffering but will work hard to reduce the effects of evil.

4

The problem of evil – summary

For the examination you should now be able to:

✔ understand how the existence of evil makes some people question the existence or the nature of God

✔ understand the different forms of evil (natural and moral) and the questions they raise about the loving nature of God

✔ know how believers explain the origins of evil and how they try to justify the continued existence of evil and suffering

✔ know and understand the free will Defence theory

✔ understand the concept of karma as an explanation for evil in the world

✔ know and be able to evaluate the responses of believers to suffering.

Sample answer

1 Write an answer to the following exam question:
Explain why natural evils call God's power into question.
(3 marks)

2 Read the following sample answer.

> Natural evils are things like volcanoes, earthquakes, droughts and tsunamis. They can have a really bad effect on people as they can destroy their houses, fields and crops and kill their children. If God made the world, then he must have allowed these evil events to happen, therefore he is to blame for them. This shows that God cannot love people or else he would not let them suffer in this way.

3 With a partner, discuss the sample answer. Do you think there are other things the student could have included in the answer?

4 What mark would you give this answer out of 3? Look at the mark scheme in the Introduction on page 7 (AO1). What are the reasons for the mark you have given?

Practice questions

1   Look at the picture below and answer the following questions.

(a) Explain how the existence of evil can make it difficult for people to understand the nature of God.   *(6 marks)*

(b) 'The stories about the origin of evil do a good job of dealing with the problem of evil.' Do you agree? Give reasons for your answer, showing that you have thought about more than one point of view.   *(6 marks)*

> **Study tip** Remember in (b) that the question is about the way the stories answer the problem of evil. There are no marks for simply retelling the stories, though you should be able to refer to points from the stories to help you illustrate your answer.

(c) (i) Explain **how** believers try to remove the effects of evil in the world.

(ii) Explain **why** believers try to remove the effects of evil in the world.   *(6 marks)*

(d) 'Human free will needs evil to exist.' Do you agree? Give reasons for your answer, showing that you have thought about more than one point of view.   *(6 marks)*

> **Study tip** Remember in (c) that you have to explain both 'how' and 'why'. Since it is a 6-mark question, you can presume that 3 marks will be for 'how' and 3 marks for 'why', so give each part equal time and weight.

5.1 The origins of the universe and the world: story of creation in Genesis 1

Introduction

Most religions have at least one story that deals with the beginnings of the universe. These stories were all written a long time ago when scientific knowledge was much less than it is today. They were probably passed down orally for some time before they were written down. Some people dismiss these stories as having no element of truth whatsoever. However, many believers feel that these stories contain essential truths that cannot be ignored. They are happy to interpret the storyline as a way of expressing a difficult topic to a non-scientific people, but what most believers would say is that the stories convey a great truth that still applies today.

It is impossible to examine all the stories of creation. To enable a reasonable study to be made, we will look at a few stories.

Objectives

Examine the story of creation in Genesis 1.

Understand what this story is trying to show about the universe and about God.

Stories in Genesis

The story in Genesis 1 is a poem based on a seven-day format (reflecting the Jewish week and showing the need for all people to have a regular day without work). The story was probably written down about 450 BCE and it reflects the idea that God is all-powerful, simply creating by his word. All things that God makes are good. Mankind is the high point of creation as everything is made ready for man.

A Genesis 1 creation story

Activities

1 Write out the main thing created on each of the first six days in two columns: days 1–3 in one column and 4–6 in the second. Here is an example of the table you should draw:

Days 1–3	Days 4–6

Examine the material in the case study on page 105 and see what it suggests to you. What message do you think the author is trying to get across?

2 'The way Genesis 1 deals with human beings shows that humans are more important than anything else.' Do you agree? Give reasons for your answer, showing that you have thought about more than one point of view.

Case study

Genesis 1 – The seven days of creation

In the beginning God created the heavens and the earth. [2]Now the earth was formless and empty, darkness was over the surface of the deep, and the Spirit of God was hovering over the waters. [3]And God said, 'Let there be light,' and there was light. [4]God saw that the light was good, and he separated the light from the darkness. [5]God called the light 'day,' and the darkness he called 'night.' And there was evening, and there was morning – the first day.

[6]And God said, 'Let there be an expanse between the waters to separate water from water.' [7]So God made the expanse and separated the water under the expanse from the water above it. And it was so. [8]God called the expanse 'sky.' And there was evening, and there was morning – the second day.

[9]And God said, 'Let the water under the sky be gathered to one place, and let dry ground appear.' And it was so. [10]God called the dry ground 'land,' and the gathered waters he called 'seas.' And God saw that it was good.

[11]Then God said, 'Let the land produce vegetation: seed-bearing plants and trees on the land that bear fruit with seed in it, according to their various kinds.' And it was so. [12]The land produced vegetation: plants bearing seed according to their kinds and trees bearing fruit with seed in it according to their kinds. And God saw that it was good. [13]And there was evening, and there was morning – the third day.

[14]And God said, 'Let there be lights in the expanse of the sky to separate the day from the night, and let them serve as signs to mark seasons and days and years, [15]and let them be lights in the expanse of the sky to give light on the earth.' And it was so. [16]God made two great lights – the greater light to govern the day and the lesser light to govern the night. He also made the stars. [17]God set them in the expanse of the sky to give light on the earth, [18]to govern the day and the night, and to separate light from darkness. And God saw that it was good. [19]And there was evening, and there was morning – the fourth day.

[20]And God said, 'Let the water teem with living creatures, and let birds fly above the earth across the expanse of the sky.' [21]So God created the great creatures of the sea and every living and moving thing with which the water teems, according to their kinds, and every winged bird according to its kind. And God saw that it was good. [22]God blessed them and said, 'Be fruitful and increase in number and fill the water in the seas, and let the birds increase on the earth.' [23]And there was evening, and there was morning – the fifth day.

[24]And God said, 'Let the land produce living creatures according to their kinds: livestock, creatures that move along the ground, and wild animals, each according to its kind.' And it was so. [25]God made the wild animals according to their kinds, the livestock according to their kinds, and all the creatures that move along the ground according to their kinds. And God saw that it was good.

[26]Then God said, 'Let us make human beings in our image, in our likeness, so that they may rule over the fish of the sea and the birds of the air, over the livestock, over all the earth, and over all the creatures that move along the ground.'

[27]So God created man in his own image, in the image of God he created him; male and female he created them.

[28]God blessed them and said to them, 'Be fruitful and increase in number; fill the earth and subdue it. Rule over the fish of the sea and the birds of the air and over every living creature that moves on the ground.'

[29]Then God said, 'I give you every seed-bearing plant on the face of the whole earth and every tree that has fruit with seed in it. They will be yours for food. [30]And to all the beasts of the earth and all the birds of the air and all the creatures that move on the ground – everything that has the breath of life in it – I give every green plant for food.' And it was so.

[31]God saw all that He had made, and it was very good. And there was evening, and there was morning – the sixth day. [2:1]Thus the heavens and the earth were completed in all their vast array. [2]By the seventh day God had finished the work he had been doing; so on the seventh day he rested from all his work. [3]And God blessed the seventh day and made it holy, because on it he rested from all the work of creating that he had done.

Genesis 1:1–2:3

Summary

You should now know that creation stories tell of the way God works as creator. Genesis 1 shows the power of God in his word and mankind as the high point of creation.

The origins of the universe and the world: other stories of creation

While the Bible stories of creation are well known in the Western world, it would be wrong to think that they are the only stories. Here are some other examples.

Case study

A Hindu story of creation

Before the creation, there was no heaven, earth or sky, only nothingness and an endless sea of darkness. A great snake floated on top of the sea, protecting within its huge and endless coils Lord Vishnu. Peace and silence reigned, and Vishnu lay still, resting in his undisturbed dreams. Suddenly, a deep humming sound began to vibrate the seas with a low Aum. The sound spread across the nothingness, rumbling and filling it with sound and motion. Vishnu awoke, sensing that the night had ended. As dawn broke, the petals of a lotus flower bloomed in Vishnu's navel, revealing Brahma sitting in the middle. Vishnu said to Brahma, 'It is time to begin'.

At Vishnu's command, a wind swept up the waters, making waves in the sea. He and the serpent vanished, leaving Brahma floating inside the lotus flower, tossed in the waves. Brahma calmed the waves and the sea by lifting up his arms. Then Brahma took the lotus flower and broke it into three pieces. One part he stretched out and made into the heavens, another part was used to create the earth, and the third part became the skies. Brahma created grasses, flowers, trees and plants to clothe the naked earth and make it beautiful. He gave each of these feeling. Next he created all kinds of animals and insects to live on the land, birds for the air and fish for the seas. To each creature he gave senses. Soon his creation was done – the air was full of sound and the earth was full of life.

Like the Genesis stories, the Hindu story reflects the idea that the gods are intimately involved in the creation. Creation is a thing of harmony and beauty, not a thing of violence and hardship. Creation is made to enable human beings to live as an integral part of the whole, not as an abuser of the gift of the gods. All creation must be treated with respect.

Research activity

Use the internet and/or a library to find a story of creation from another religion or an ancient myth. What is this story saying about creation? How does this creation story compare to those mentioned in this book?

A *Lord Vishnu*

Sikh story of creation

For infinite ages before the world was created, darkness reigned. The earth and sky did not yet exist. There was no moon or sun to give light, no day or night to break the blankness. All was still and quiet, as a deep, undisturbed meditation.

However, the universe did not spring into being on its own. There was a Creator. The True Lord created air and other gases, and from the air came water, and from water he created three worlds ('three worlds' is a metaphor or common term for the entire universe and all within it). The Light of the Creator was placed in every single heart.

B   *The Guru Granth Sahib, the holy scripture of Sikhism*

Josie is a 44 year old Jewess. She says: 'For me G-d made everything. There is nothing that exists without his power and his will. However, how he made things is unknown to human beings. We were not there so we have no idea of the actual process. I am happy to accept what scientists tell us about their discoveries. But this does not stop me valuing the creation stories. I do not think that the creation stories give any factual account of what happened. What they do give is an insight into how people have responded to the idea of G-d as the creator and the peace, beauty and harmony that underlie all things. These stories give us a very good idea of the quality of what G-d has created, not the manner in which he created.'

What do you think of Josie's ideas?

Discussion activity

As a class, debate the topic: 'Creation stories have nothing to offer people in the 21st century.'

Extension activity

Write a story about creation to tell to young people. The story needs to give them some idea of the beauty and harmony of creation and also to entertain them. What similarities and differences are there between your attempts and the stories of creation that you have already looked at?

Summary

You should now recognise that accounts of creation are often in the form of a story. Most believers do not take these as literal truth. Most creation stories focus on the qualities of God as shown through his creative power and on the role of humanity as an essential part of creation.

Activities

1   Either draw a strip cartoon to show one of the above stories or write a poem to reflect the content of the story.

2   'The most important thing about creation is that it is a gift from God.' Do you agree? Give reasons for your answer, showing that you have thought about more than one point of view.

3   'No account of creation should be taken seriously.' Do you agree? Give reasons for your answer, showing that you have thought about more than one point of view.

5.3 The origins of the universe and the world: stories of creation in fundamentalism

Fundamentalists

Who are fundamentalists?

Within all religions there are different groups that claim that they are following the religion in the way that God or the founder wanted them to do so. They are often called fundamentalists, as they claim that they are going back to the fundamental principles of their religion. They will reject any attempt, as they see it, to corrupt the religion. Most of these groups reflect a conservative or right-wing approach to the religion. This applies in particular to matters of authority.

How do fundamentalists use religious texts?

In most religions the central source of authority is a sacred text, though some religions combine the authority of the sacred text with a group or an individual whose role it is to interpret that text. Many of these groups take the view that the sacred text is holy because it comes from God and that no human being can reject what the sacred text contains. This applies to many aspects of the texts and of life.

There are groups of Muslims who say that every word in the Qur'an is to be followed, including the punishments for offences laid down in it. There are some Hindus who reject anything that is not part of the original Vedic texts. Among the most active fundamentalist groups are Christian fundamentalists. They take a strict approach to the creation stories. By looking at their approach to the Genesis stories you can get a good feel for all fundamentalist positions.

The fundamentalist approach to the Genesis stories

Some Christians who take the fundamentalist approach would say that the Holy Spirit almost dictated the Bible and that no one should question anything that the Bible teaches. This approach is based on the idea that God is the God of truth and that he would not mislead people in any way. As the Bible is God's word, it contains nothing but the truth. This type of fundamentalist would claim that no human being is in a position to question anything that God has said. However, they might be willing to accept, for instance, that a day in Genesis 1 does not mean exactly a 24 hour period. Fundamentalists would say that where there are apparent contradictions, people do not yet have enough understanding, either of the text or of truth.

An extreme form of fundamentalism is literalism. Literalism takes the view that every word recorded in the Bible is true as it stands. For example, on Genesis 1 they would say that God actually made the world in six lots of 24 hours (one Anglican bishop once worked out that man was created at 9 a.m. on 23 October 4004 BC) and that Noah actually took two of every animal into the ark to save them from dying in the flood.

Objectives

Understand what is meant by fundamentalism.

Examine how fundamentalists approach the creation stories.

Key terms

Fundamentalist: a person who believes in the basics of a religion, particularly believing that what is contained in the sacred text is an accurate, almost factual, record that cannot be questioned.

Study tip

For a fundamentalist approach, think of each creation story as a factual account.

Research activity

Use the internet and/or a library to find out all you can about a fundamentalist group in a religion other than Christianity.

∞ links

For more about evolution and how it relates to religious beliefs, see pages 116–119.

Activity

Give two arguments in favour of a fundamentalist approach to interpreting the Bible and two arguments against this approach.

A *How would a fundamentalist explain the story of Noah's ark?*

The fundamentalist approach rejects any form of compromise with science. If an idea is not contained in the Bible or if it contradicts the Bible, then the idea cannot be the truth. God has communicated to people everything that they need to know about himself and life. If people are not prepared to accept what God has to say, that is not God's fault, it is their own. Fundamentalists would argue that God is the direct creator of everything as it is. Evolution, as modern Darwinists would teach it, did not happen.

Discussion activity

Divide into two groups and debate the following: 'This house believes that the creation stories in Genesis are a true account of what happened at creation.'

Case study

Stephen is a 35 year old Christian fundamentalist. He says: 'The Bible is the word of God. God will not tell us a lie as he cannot be untruthful to himself. Every word that God wants us to know, he has given to us. We are in no position to challenge the truth that comes from God. All that the Bible contains is true and it is all that is needed for salvation. Anything else or any interpretation of the Bible that changes the meaning from what God actually says, can only come from the Devil, the Prince of lies, the great deceiver. Human minds might appear to be great, but they are only creations of God. No human mind can question what God knows as it is only a small part of God's great creation. If humans are humble and accept their own limitations, they might find they are more in harmony with God, with each other and with nature'.

Summary

You should now understand that the Bible accounts are historical records as far as Christian fundamentalists are concerned. Fundamentalists accept that each part of the sacred text is from God so cannot be changed.

The origins of the universe and the world: the big bang and other scientific theories

Scientific theories about the beginning of the universe

The big bang theory

The most popularly held scientific theory about the origins of the universe is called the **big bang theory**. This theory arose as a result of various observations made about the universe, in particular:

- galaxies far away from our own galaxy, the Milky Way are getting further away from us
- as the galaxies are moving away, the whole universe is getting cooler
- there is a noise that is the same at every part of the universe and which is the result of a great explosion.

A *Does the Big Bang theory explain the creation of the universe?*

These factors led to the belief that all the matter in the universe was once an infinitely compact fireball. The matter that makes up the universe was, at one time, all squashed together, and it was so dense and hot that it could no longer keep itself together. The matter exploded, and after it did so it started to cool. This probably took place nearly 15 billion years ago.

As space and time were created in this big bang, the temperature gradually decreased from billions of degrees Celsius to the present temperature, and elements such as helium and hydrogen were formed. Slowly, islands of more solid matter formed and these gradually combined to form billions of galaxies, each containing billions of stars of all sizes. These form the universe we know today.

The oldest star in our Milky Way is probably 13.2 billion years old. Our solar system probably started to form about 4.6 billion years ago, with the sun exploding into light about 100 million years after that.

The steady state theory

An alternative to the Big Bang theory is the steady state theory. This theory accepts the fact that the universe is expanding, but it believes that the universe itself is infinite in time. Physicists such as Fred Hoyle would claim that there is a limited amount of matter in the universe and that it is changing in form, so when a sun explodes, the energy that is released can become other aspects of the universe. According to this theory, we do not need to think about a starting point for the universe. All we need to do is to accept that changes in the nature of the universe are always happening and that matter and energy are just different forms of the same thing. Not many scientists agree with the steady state theory, but it does show that not every scientist accepts the big bang theory.

▆ What do these theories suggest about the universe?

Many of the scientific descriptions of the origins of the universe seem to suggest that things just happened by themselves. Certainly, once a start had been made, whether as a result of a 'big bang', or simply because things have always existed, it is possible to see the universe following an almost inevitable course as a result of the laws of science and of nature. Although some scientists believe that these theories allow for the belief that God created the universe, they could also make sense without a God.

These theories also raise questions about the end of the universe and, almost inevitably, the destiny of man:

- Some scientists think that the universe will simply carry on growing until everything is stretched so thinly that it evaporates into nothing.
- Some scientists think that the universe will reach a point of maximum expansion and then will collapse in on itself, creating a 'big crunch', which might later lead to the next big bang.
- What seems inevitable for humanity is that in the relatively near future (the next 5 billion years or so) the sun will become a red giant that will have swallowed the earth, so life on earth will not be able to be sustained.

Activity

2 What problems are raised by having more than one scientific theory about the origins of the universe proposed by scientists?

Study tip

Remember that this is a religious studies exam and not a science exam. You only need to be aware of the general points about the scientific theories and what questions they raise about the role of God in creation. You do not need to be able to quote all the scientific facts.

Summary

You should now know that scientific theories about the beginning of the universe include the big bang theory and the steady state theory. People have different views on whether science has given us enough evidence to explain why things exist and whether belief in God can be held together with belief in a scientific theory.

Activities

3 How important do you think that scientific theories about the universe are for humanity? Explain your answer.

4 'Life is just a coincidence.' Do you agree? Give reasons for your answer, showing that you have thought about more than one point of view.

5 'It is quite possible to accept the big bang theory and believe in a God who created the world.' Do you agree? Give reasons for your answer, showing that you have thought about more than one point of view.

God and the religious stories

The stories of creation (for example, Genesis 1 and 2, the Hindu story) were told by ordinary people, in a non-scientific age to help their own generation understand something about the nature of life and the universe. The originators of these stories felt that God was the creator and that God had a special role for humanity to play within the world. The stories that evolved focus on this relationship of God and humanity within creation. These stories were trying to find a meaning behind creation; what creation shows about God. They were not written to present a factual account of historical events and it would be wrong to read them in that light. For most believers the underlying message is true, regardless of the historical details.

- God made everything.
- God made everything good.
- Humanity is the highest point of creation.

If there is no God, then arguably life has no value, humanity has no value and creation has no value. The religious stories of creation stress the need for people to respect all that has been made.

Activities

1. What did the authors of religious stories about creation aim to do in their stories?

2. 'It is wrong to see the religious stories about creation as historical facts.' Do you agree? Give reasons for your answer, showing that you have thought about more than one point of view.

Extension activity

Use the internet and/or a library to research some scientific theories that were popular for a long time but which have since been shown to be false. What does this suggest about scientific theories? Does this have anything to offer to the debate about the role of God and scientific theories regarding creation? Explain your answer.

Case study

Ramul is a scientist who believes that there is a God. He says: 'For me, there is absolutely no tension between what science has to offer and the fact of God's existence. Science is very good at looking at what happens in the world and the universe. It can show how things occur and it can show us the relationships between most aspects of life, even if some of the final pieces of evidence have yet to be found. Scientists for the most part accept that some things are too small to be able to fully demonstrate them or too complex to be able to explain them to anyone who has not had a detailed scientific training. However, the one thing science cannot do is to explain why there is anything at all. Science comes into its own domain when it is dealing with what has already come into existence, but it is unable to give any answer about why thing exist. This question belongs to theology, not science.'

What do you think about Ramul's thoughts? Explain your answer.

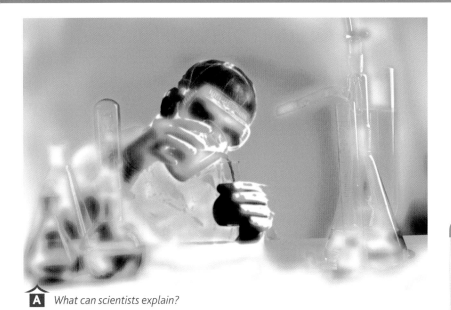

A *What can scientists explain?*

God and the scientific theories

Some people think that because scientists can explain the steps taken to find the theories that they come up with, the scientists have to be fully correct. Others would point out, however, that all science is based on ideas that are seeking support. At times, evidence that does not fully fit in with scientific theory may be ignored or set aside.

Some people think that science can provide all the answers, especially if the scientists are given enough time to do the research properly. They believe that there will then be no 'need' for God – everything will be explained without him. There are many reputable scientists, however, who are firm believers in God and do not see any contradiction in their position. They believe that God is the creator of a universe which could well have been created following a big bang.

Science can usually provide very good explanations of how things happen. The role of science is mainly to describe observable events and to link them together. Science cannot easily explain why things happen unless there is a direct, observable connection between two stages, and one is clearly seen to be causing the other.

Many believers are happy to accept the idea of the big bang theory (or even the steady state theory, though this is not very popular at the moment). Most believers do not find that their belief in God as the creator is affected by these scientific theories. A common question asked by believers is: where did the material that created the big bang come from? Or if there is an infinite universe, where did the matter that makes up the universe come from? Many believers are happy with the idea that God could have created the universe through the big bang. To pretend that the big bang explains everything in such a way that there is no need for God would appear to be unsatisfactory to many believers.

Summary

You should now understand that many scientists are believers and many believers accept the scientific theories about creation and believe in a creator God. Many believers think God may have created through the processes described by scientific theories. For them the ideas of God and the scientific theories do not contradict each other.

Charles Darwin

Charles Darwin (1808–1882) worked as a naturalist on board *HMS Beagle* during a voyage from 1831–1836. During this time, Darwin spent a long time studying the animals and birds on the Galapagos Islands, 1,000 miles from the coast of South America. During his studies, Darwin noticed major differences in some of the animals, especially the finches found on the various islands. Some of the finches had short, heavy bills while others had thin, delicate bills with other varieties being variations on these. Darwin came up with the idea that the characteristic that enabled the finches and the other animals to feed, breed and survive best would be passed on to future generations of the bird or animal.

Darwin published a book called *On the Origin of Species by* means of Natural Selection in 1859. A book applying the theory to human beings, called *The Descent of Man* was published in 1871. At this time many Christians rejected Darwin's theories because they felt they went against the teachings of the Bible and they undermined the importance of humanity.

A A memorial to Charles Darwin

Evolution

The theory of **evolution** states that plant and animal life developed gradually from primitive life forms and that species adapts to their environment.

Objectives

Know and understand what Charles Darwin taught about evolution.

Understand why this theory is seen as a challenge by some believers.

Evaluate the acceptability of the idea of evolution.

Research activity 🔍

1   Use the Internet and/or a library to find out five facts about Charles Darwin and his writings beyond those facts given in the above paragraph.

Activity

1   Why did many believers react angrily to Darwin's theories?

Key terms

Evolution: the process made popular by Charles Darwin that describes hoe simpler life-forms gradually changed and adapted to more complex life forms.

Case study

The peppered moth

A simple example of this is the peppered moth. The peppered moth comes in both a pale variety and a dark variety and they rest on birch trees. Before the Industrial Revolution, the colour of birch trees was pale so the dark peppered moths stood out and were easily spotted and eaten by predators. This meant that the pale variety of peppered moth flourished. During the Industrial Revolution, the trees became covered in soot and became darker, so the pale moths stood out and they were eaten, meaning the dark moths flourished. Nowadays the trees are clean again and the paler moths are once again flourishing.

Examples like the one in the case study can be found the natural world. The theory of evolution states that life started with simple organisms and then over long periods of time became more complex. Whenever a change gave an organism an advantage in a particular environment it meant that the genes of that organism would be more likely to pass on to the next generation and the offspring would have the same advantage which might be passed on to the next generation. Darwin called this process 'natural selection'. It is often called 'the survival of fittest' because creatures that are most fit for their lifestyle are the ones that survive'.

Fossil records do contain a large number of species that have not survived, but they can also indicate earlier forms of animals that have survived in a mutated (changed) form. Unfortunately, evolution takes a long time to happen, with few cases being as obvious as the peppered moth. However, DNA research does seem to suggest that there are close similarities between many species, which reinforces the idea of evolution.

Does evolution take place?

Arguments against evolution

Some people question the validity of the idea of evolution. They question whether the gaps in the fossil records show that there ever were any missing links. Evolution is so slow that it cannot be seen to be taking place. This means that the evidence is all presupposition and interpretation of incomplete material.

Some people would argue that the forms of animals that exist now and the complexity of many of their organs would suggest special creation, not haphazard evolution.

Some believers would argue that the theory of evolution undermines the role of a perfect God. In Genesis, for instance, the emphasis is on God who made everything perfect from the start. They suggest that if God did not make everything perfect, as he wanted it to be, then God himself is not perfect and therefore is limited and not God. They reject the idea that God would allow his creation to be changed drastically from what he wanted it to be.

Some fundamentalist believers hold the view that evolution is not mentioned in the sacred texts. Therefore, it did not take place.

Religious arguments for evolution

Many believers, however, are happy to accept the theory of evolution. They think God could have used evolution to create animals. They accept that there is sufficient evidence for evolution and do not question the ability of God to work in this way.

Summary

You should now know and understand that Charles Darwin proposed the theory of evolution based on the differences and similarities that he noted between animals of the same species. Many believers see no problem with the idea of God working through evolution. Other believers reject the idea of evolution as it goes against the sacred texts, claiming that the evidence for the theory is not strong.

Research activity

2   Choose one animal and use the internet and/or a library to discover what scientists think it has evolved from.

Activity

2   'There is not enough evidence to support the idea of evolution.' What do you think? Explain your opinion.

Study tip

Try to think about these arguments in a non-biased way to get a feel for what the different views are, with their strengths and weaknesses.

Extension activity

Choose one of the arguments against evolution and find evidence either to attack or to defend this argument.

Activities

3   State two arguments for and two arguments against believers accepting the idea of creation through evolution.

4   'To say that God cannot work through evolution would be to limit God.' Do you agree? Give reasons for your answer, showing that you have thought about more than one point of view.

The implications of the Darwinian view of evolution for the place of humanity in creation

The evolution of humanity

According to Darwin's theory of evolution, all animals have come from a common starting point. As genetic changes took place and as animals responded to the changing conditions, the different species emerged. Human beings are just one of these different species.

Genetic studies show that chimpanzees and human beings had a common ancestor that lived in Africa about 7.5 million years ago. This ancestor's descendants split into two different lines: chimpanzees and human beings. However, this separation of the species took a very long time to complete. Humans only began to look as they do today about 200,000 years ago (compare to the start of the earth 4.54 billion years ago and the extinction of the land dinosaurs about 65 million years ago).

Know and understand what the Darwinian view of evolution might say about human beings.

Understand why this view is a challenge to believers' ideas about the human condition.

Assess the validity of both sides of this argument.

A *Human evolution*

The implications of the Darwinian theory for humanity

Negative implications

If the **Darwinian view** is correct, many people would state that some, if not all, of the following statements must be true about humans:

- humans are simply another, though slightly more advanced, form of animals
- the creation of human beings was just a lucky genetic mutation
- humans have no more right to be on the earth than any other animals
- in comparison to the dinosaurs (who dominated the earth for about 160 million years) humans have little importance
- human life probably has no value apart from the very short time each individual is alive.

Key terms

Darwinian view: named after Charles Darwin who pioneered the idea of evolution; the idea that creatures have gradually changed and adapted to suit the environment, 'the survival of the fittest.'

This approach could create a negative attitude to humanity and to a person's own life. However, many people believe that the human race is so far above the other animals that humans are of a special order. They would say that there has been such a leap in creation, even through evolution, that it is wrong to limit human beings in this negative way.

Activities

1. Try to complete a timeline or a 24-hour clock from the moment of the big bang to today. Notice how recent human beings are in the whole process of creation.

2. Consider whether the recent creation of humanity suggests anything about the role and value of humanity.

3. Look at the statements in the bulleted list above. Explain which ones you agree with and which ones you disagree with.

4. 'The Darwinian theory of evolution gives little value to the individual human being.' Do you agree? Give reasons for your answer, showing that you have thought about more than one point of view.

5. 'Every individual is important simply because he or she is alive.' Do you agree? Give reasons for your answer, showing that you have thought about more than one point of view.

Discussion activity

As a class, debate the topic: 'Human beings are nothing more than animals.'

Positive implications

Some people would claim that each human being is important because what matters is the race as a whole, and each person contributes to the race by passing on his or her genes. This approach is more focused on the group aspect of the human race, but it is also stressing the fact that every individual is essential within the human race. One way to think about it could be that evolution has been leading up to me and will go out from me. This might seem to be a self-centred approach to understanding evolution, but it is at least acknowledging that I have a real reason to be here and this should not be denied me.

Following on from that, it could be argued that the way I treat each individual is important because I am recognising the value of the human race as a whole, rather than of each individual. While one person's life and purpose might end at death, that life is important while that person is alive.

Summary

You should now know and understand that according to Darwin's theory, humans have evolved from lower forms of animals. Some people would claim that humans do not have any special value in creation. Other people would argue that each individual has value simply as a member of the human race.

Study tip

Look at the general pattern of ideas which affect religious belief rather than going into the scientific details.

The contrasting view of the role of humanity as shown in creation stories

Beliefs in monotheistic religions

Judaism, Christianity and Islam all share a common understanding of the role of the human race in creation. This understanding is reflected in and built on the creation stories of Genesis 1 and 2. The central features of the religions' attitude to humanity are:

- humans are made in the image and likeness of God, which means that the qualities that make humans different are reflections of God's qualities (for example, love and knowledge)
- humans share in the life force (breath) of God in a way the other animals do not
- humans have the command from God to multiply and fill the earth
- humans are given free will which is not given to any other animal
- humans have power over the animals – this is shown by the way Adam names each animal
- along with power over the animals, humans have the duty to care for the earth and all creatures. Humans are stewards of creation
- humans are the only animal that God has made a covenant with.

Objectives

Study what religious stories show about the role of humans in creation.

Understand how religions give a greater dignity to the human race.

Evaluate the religious and Darwinian views of the role of humanity.

∞ **links**

See pages 104–107 to read the stories of creation mentioned here.

Beliefs and teachings

For Sikhs, '*The Lord infused his light into the dust and created the universe*' *(Guru Granth Sahib)*. Humans have the tasks of living in harmony with nature and achieving a state of bliss in creation.

A *Humans have a duty to care for animals*

Activities

1. Examine each statement in the list above. Which ones do you agree with and which ones do you disagree with? Why?

2. 'For the monotheistic religions humanity is almost like God.' Do you agree? Give reasons for your answer, showing that you have thought about more than one point of view.

Beliefs in Hinduism and Buddhism

Eastern religions, particularly Buddhism and Hinduism, believe in some type of reincarnation or rebirth. For human beings, life is about doing well and building up good karma. Humans are on the higher plane of life, which allows them to make choices and to live with the results of their choices. This means that the quality of life is much more fulfilling for humans than it is for animals. Animals cannot escape the cycle of rebirth or reincarnation, whereas humans have this possibility. Those humans who live a poor quality life might come back in an animal form, suggesting that animal existence is thought to be below human existence.

As the world and this life are thought of basically as illusions, scientific theories such as evolution have little sway with Buddhists or Hindus. Both religions accept the need to reach beyond the immediate, so the value of the human being is in how he or she deals with life now, not worrying about what theoretical value any scientific theory might give to human life. For Buddhists, human beings are part of the creation that is in a constant state of becoming and so nothing has fixed value, only potential.

Beliefs and teachings

[4] What is man that you are mindful of him, the son of man that you care for him?

[5] You made him a little lower than the heavenly beings and crowned him with glory and honour.

[6] You made him ruler over the works of your hands; you put everything under his feet:

Psalms 8:4-6

Activities

3   Do you think that human beings have more or less value in Hinduism/Buddhism or in Judaism/Christianity/Islam? Explain your answer.

4   'Science and religion both give human beings an important role in the universe.' Do you agree? Give reasons for your answer, showing that you have thought about more than one point of view.

∞ links

See page 130 for Reincarnation and rebirth.

Case study

Sita is a 24 year old Hindu. She says: 'All animals need to be treated with respect as they are part of this created order. Humans are special because of our extra intelligence and our ability to make real decisions that affect our karma and reincarnation. I would not want to be badly treated as a human being so I must not treat any animal badly. I try to show respect for everything as a way of showing my thanks for being alive. This includes not treating animals badly. However, human beings must be treated with even greater respect. If I do this then hopefully I will be fulfilling my function as a human being in this incarnation.'

Summary

You should now understand that in Judaism, Christianity, Islam and Sikhism, humanity has an important role and a special place in creation. Most religions believe that humans are more than just well-evolved animals and that they have a duty to care for the earth and to develop themselves fully.

Study tip

To help you understand these views, think what the world would be like if human beings were simply mindless animals.

5.9   Fundamentalist views on evolution

Fundamentalists

Fundamentalists are believers who accept that the teachings handed down from the past are literal and scientific truth. In the matter of evolution, the strongest fundamentalist reaction has come from some Christian and some Jewish believers so these will be the groups that will be discussed here.

There are two major approaches to evolution taken by fundamentalists:

- to accept that everything written in the Bible is correct
- to support the idea of Intelligent Design.

The correctness of scripture

Many fundamentalists believe that what is presented in the *Bible*, particularly in Genesis 1–3, is an accurate record of events, though some would accept that the word 'day' does not mean literally 24 hours. This approach means that God made each animal as a specific creation. This applied in particular to human beings. Evolution is seen as contradicting the word of God in creating different creatures, for example, God said 'let the land produce living creatures … and it was so.' So it is rejected by these believers. They believe that the words contained in the Bible are given by God and therefore should be regarded as providing scientific truth. They believe that God cannot lie and accept this view of the creation of the world. Some fundamentalists would argue that God has let people know all the truth and there is no need to go searching for anything else.

Intelligent design

In the last 20 years or so a development has taken place that is called the intelligent design movement. This is a group of fundamentalist believers who accept that the biblical accounts of creation are basically true, but they also accept that there have been changes and mutations in the animal kingdom over the ages. The intelligent design movement rejects any idea of random (chance) mutations that bring about fortunate improvements for creation. They believe that God can work through these changes, that God actually directs these changes to bring variations in creation. God is the intelligence behind the design, the one who is driving changes forward.

Objectives

Examine what fundamentalists would say about the theory of evolution.

Understand why they hold this viewpoint.

Assess the relevance of this viewpoint for the 21st century.

Extension activity

1 Examine the beliefs of those who say that scripture contains all the knowledge that humans need. What is your attitude to this belief? Explain your answer.

A *God is the intelligent designer*

Extension activity

2 Study the evidence that could be used against the process of evolution, especially in the light of the Bible stories. Do you think that evolution has all the answers to the mysteries of creation? Explain your answer.

Activities

1. Explain the differences between believers in intelligent design and believers in the correctness of scripture.

2. 'Intelligent design makes sense of evolution.' What do you think? Explain your opinion.

Research activity

Use the internet and/or a library to study the work of Richard Dawkins on evolution. Are you convinced by his ideas? Explain your answer.

Case study

Intelligent Design is based on scientific research. Those who hold this view claim that there are many life-forms whose basic structure is extremely complex. They say that this could not have occurred accidentally or through evolution but must be down to a creator. There seems to be a pattern in many parts of living creation that reflects genuine design. Such design has to come from a designer who had a purpose behind his creation.

Some people say that the theory of Intelligent Design is an attempt, by those who believe in the accuracy of the accounts of creation in Genesis, to get their ideas accepted by the scientific community, by simply rephrasing their thoughts. In response, those who believe in intelligent design refer to scientific studies. They say it would be wrong to dismiss all the scientific evidence that supports changes through evolution. However, evolution cannot explain everything. Allowing for God to act through nature to move things along or to place things on a particular course seems to unite the best aspects of faith and science.

Study tip

The best way to understand the views of fundamentalists is to start by accepting, at least for a time, that the accounts of creation in the Bible are correct.

Extension activity

3. Study the work of Richard Dawkins on evolution. Are you convinced by his ideas? Explain your answer.

Discussion activity

As a class, debate the topic: 'There is too much evidence in favour of evolution for believers to ignore this theory.'

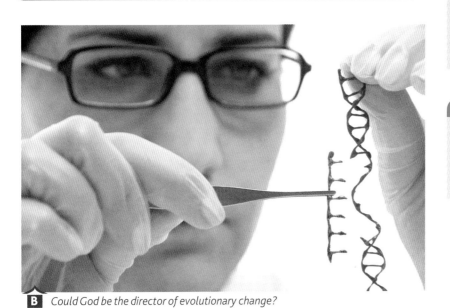

B   *Could God be the director of evolutionary change?*

Summary

You should now understand that some believers insist that evolution rejects the teachings of the Bible in relation to creation. They cannot accept evolution as a true account of how life developed. The intelligent design movement believes that God drives the changes in the way that he wants. So God works through evolution directly.

5

The compatibility of religion and science – summary

For the examination, you should now be able to:

✔ understand religious and scientific explanations about creation

✔ know and understand interpretations of some stories of creation and the role of God in creation according to these different view

✔ know and understand the Big Bang and other scientific theories about the origins of the universe

✔ understand religious and Darwinian views about humanity and its place in creation

✔ evaluate whether the views of religion and science are compatible

✔ know and explain the contrasting view of the role of humanity as shown in Creation stories

✔ understand the fundamentalist views on evolution.

Sample answer

1 Write an answer to the following exam question:
Explain why fundamentalists question the idea of evolution.

(4 marks)

2 Read the following sample answer.

> Fundamentalists take the line that God has told them everything that they need to know about the world and life. They believe that scientists have rejected God's message as passed on in books like the Bible and so they are not willing to give any scientific ideas any weight. Evolution says that man came from lower animals, which would question the idea that God put His spirit into man.

3 With a partner, discuss the sample answer. Do you think there are other things the student could have included in the answer?

4 What mark would you give this answer out of 4? Look at the mark scheme in the Introduction on page 7 (AO1). What are the reasons for the mark you have given?

Practice questions

1   Look at the picture below and answer the following questions.

(a) Describe how science explains the origins of the universe.   *(6 marks)*

(b) 'Science leaves no room for God in creation.' Do you agree? Give reasons for
     your answer, showing that you have thought about more than one point of view.   *(6 marks)*

(c) Explain how religious accounts of creation give humanity a special place.   *(6 marks)*

(d) 'Evolution does not treat humanity as special.' Do you agree? Give reasons for
     your answer, showing that you have thought about more than one point of view.
     Refer to religious arguments in your answer.   *(6 marks)*

Study tip   Remember in (b) and (d) that you have to include religious viewpoints and arguments.

6.1 Evidence for and against an afterlife

Introduction

Nearly all religions have a belief in a life after death. These beliefs take one of two basic forms:

- the soul of the dead person enters a new, eternal state of happiness with God or punishment
- the soul of the dead person is reborn or reincarnated to come back to another earthly existence.

In general, the belief in the eternal continuation of the individual's soul is held by Jews, Christians and Muslims. Belief in reincarnation is held by Hindus and belief in rebirth by Buddhists. Within all these groups of believers there are minor, and at times major, differences, but this chapter will outline the main beliefs.

Why people believe in an afterlife

Belief in some kind of continued existence after death has been about since the earliest stages of civilisation, as is shown by the care taken over burials among the ancient peoples. This probably reflects a sense that a life that is only available for a short time, even if that were 90 years, would seem pointless and wasteful. Consider the following opinions.

- Life often seems unfair – some of those who are good die young or suffer, some who do bad things prosper. There might be little point in trying to live a good life if good and bad people ended their life and there was nothing more.
- People seem to be aware of a deeper aspect to life. Why would this happen if there is nothing there to raise this awareness?
- Don't things like dreams, extrasensory perception, etc. suggest that there is more to the individual than just the flesh?
- When a person dies the physical body remains, but there is obviously something missing from it – the spark of life or what some people refer to as the soul. What happens to the soul?

Objectives

Know and understand the evidence offered for the existence of an afterlife.

Understand the limitations of such evidence.

Evaluate the evidence offered for the existence of an afterlife.

⚭ links

To find out more about reincarnation and rebirth, see pages 130–131.

Activity

1. Draw up a chart that shows which believers hold what views about life after death.

A *Why do people take such care of the dead?*

Activities

2 Look at the four statements in the bulleted list on page 124 and say what you think about each one. How strong is the argument for life after death in each statement you choose?

3 'People only believe in a life after death because they are scared of becoming nothing at death.' Do you agree? Give reasons for your answer, showing that you have thought about more than one point of view.

Evidence for and against the existence of an afterlife

There is very little solid evidence either for or against an afterlife. If there was any definite evidence, the issue would not raise so many problems and differences of opinion. The type of evidence people refer to, to support their own position, might include some of the following, dependent on the actual view being put forward:

- the existence of ghosts, spectres, hauntings, etc
- the Resurrection of Jesus as witnessed in the Bible
- the way some people claim to remember events from a previous life
- out-of-body and near-death experiences
- the teachings of the Qur'an.

Many people believe that something happens to people after death and yet they accept that there is no solid evidence for this belief. This is why it is a matter of Faith. The evidence is weak (or even, some would say, non-existent) and yet believers accept that their life continues in some way. This belief shapes their understanding of the value of life itself: what they are prepared to put up with in their life, what they are prepared to accept death (martyrdom) for, how they respond when someone close to them dies. While some people may present fairly strong arguments against any continuation of life beyond the grave, believers find it impossible to reject their inner conviction (their faith) about this topic.

Research activity

Choose one religion and use the internet and/or a library to examine how believers of that religion would treat a dead body. What does this suggest about the beliefs in life after death in that religion?

⊙⊙ links

For a definition of resurrection, see page 126.

Activity

4 Go through each of these pieces of evidence and say how strong each one is as evidence for life after death. Explain your answers.

Activity

5 'Faith removes any doubts about the existence of life after death.' Do you agree? Give reasons for your answer, showing that you have thought about more than one point of view.

Extension activity

1 Use the internet and/or a library to compare the ways the dead are treated today with how the dead were treated in one ancient society. What similarities and differences do you notice?

Extension activity

2 Do you think that the changes in the way the dead are treated reflect practical concerns or deeper theological or philosophical concerns? Explain your answer.

Summary

You should now know that nearly all religions have some teaching about an afterlife. There are various ideas about what happens in this afterlife. The evidence for the existence of life after death is not strong, but there are a number of arguments that are used to suggest that life makes more sense if there is an afterlife. Life after death is a matter of belief not knowledge.

Eternal life

Eternal life

Eternal life refers to the belief that a person who lives on earth now will die but, after death, will enter an unending state in which the identity of the person continues. Eternal life is a reward for living a good life on earth. It means being with God forever. For believers, this reward does not come to everybody. Those who reject God and live bad lives will face eternal punishment in hell or some similar state.

The idea of eternal life is built on an awareness of the love of God. Believers accept that God creates people out of love. If people cease to be at the moment of death, this would suggest that God's creation has no purpose and that it shows no love for what God has created. This would in itself raise questions about God: how can God love people into being and then let them cease to be? Most believers accept that God's love is eternal. If he creates in love, then that creation must also be eternal. If God only creates for a short time that would suggest that God is changeable and limited; and if God is limited then he is not perfect and therefore he is not God. God must love the individual forever.

Death cannot then be the end of the individual. While the body might be left behind (like the butterfly emerging from the chrysalis created by the caterpillar), the innermost being of the individual (sometimes called the soul) must continue for ever.

Resurrection

In the early Jewish scriptures, the belief was that when people died they all entered Sheol, a place where all the dead would go, but in which people had no direct contact with God. Gradually, there arose the idea that God would restore to life those who had been faithful to him. When this resurrection would happen was open to question. Some people believed that when the Messiah appeared, the just would be rewarded. Other people thought that the reward would happen at the end of time. What was important was the belief that the reward would happen. For most Jews, this included the belief that the physical body would be restored to the faithful.

This restoring to life meant that the person would come back to an endless happy state in the presence of God. At the same time there was a growth in the idea that the wicked would be punished. Some Jews still believe in this, but some Jews state that the soul will continue without a body.

Jesus' resurrection

Jesus was a Jew who referred in his teachings to the Kingdom of God, sometimes called the Kingdom of Heaven, and the sufferings of hell – an existence without God. Jesus believed that God's love reached beyond death. The underlying idea is that God had created the world to be a perfect place and this had been destroyed by sin and the power of evil. Once sin and death are defeated, the whole of creation would become as perfect as God had intended them to be. By his death and resurrection, Jesus defeated the power of sin and death.

Objectives

Know and understand what believers mean by resurrection.

Understand the effect of this belief on believers.

Evaluate the validity of this belief.

Activities

1 Explain what is meant by eternal life.

2 'If what believers say about God is true, there must be eternal life.' Do you agree? Give reasons for your answer, showing that you have thought about more than one point of view.

Key terms

Eternal life: everlasting life after death.

Resurrection: the Christian belief that Jesus rose from the dead and entered into eternal life and that all souls will join in this resurrection on the Last Day.

Beliefs and teachings

The central point of Christianity is the teaching about Jesus' resurrection. As it says in 1 *Corinthians* 15:12–19:

^{12}'But if it is preached that Christ has been raised from the dead, how can some of you say that there is no resurrection of the dead? ^{13}If there is no resurrection of the dead, then not even Christ has been raised. ^{14}And if Christ has not been raised, our preaching is useless and so is your faith. ^{15}More than that, we are then found to be false witnesses about God, for we have testified about God that he raised Christ from the dead. But he did not raise him if in fact the dead are not raised. ^{16}For if the dead are not raised, then Christ has not been raised either. ^{17}And if Christ has not been raised, your faith is futile; you are still in your sins. ^{18}Then those also who have fallen asleep in Christ are lost. ^{19}If only for this life we have hope in Christ, we are to be pitied more than all men.'

Christians believe that Jesus really died but that, on the third day, the tomb in which he had been placed was empty. At first the disciples could not believe the message of the women that they had seen Jesus alive, but when they personally experienced Jesus, touched him and ate with him they were convinced that he had defeated death.

Christians believe that, through the death and resurrection of Jesus, all people have access to God in heaven. What has happened to Jesus will happen to all who accept the love of God shown in Jesus – they will be resurrected to eternal life.

Through resurrection, the body is transformed. It loses its previous limitations and achieves a glorious state. Yet the persons who lived before dying are still really present in a more perfect form of themselves. In other words, Christians believe that God recreates fully; He completes His creation.

Activities

3   Why do you think people rejected the idea of Sheol?

4   Why is Jesus' resurrection so important for Christians? (Refer to the extract from 1 Corinthians 15 above.)

5   Draw a caterpillar, a chrysalis and a butterfly. In what ways do these drawings reflect what is taught about resurrection?

6   'Jesus' resurrection proves that there is life after death.' Do you agree? Give reasons for your answer, showing that you have thought about more than one point of view.

Summary

You should now understand that eternal life is the continuation of the existence of the individual, in a perfect, form for all eternity. Resurrection means that the whole person will be raised to new life, following the example of Jesus.

Extension activity

1   Examine the following passages from the Jewish Bible and the Deutero-canonical books. What do they show about a developing understanding about life after death? Psalm 115:17-18, Isaiah 38:16-19, Job 19:25-27, 2 Maccabees 7:1-42, Daniel 12:1-3.

Extension activity

2   Examine the following passages from the Christian Bible. What do they show about Christian beliefs in the resurrection? John 20:1-29, 1 Thessalonians 4:16-18, 1 Corinthians 15:39-53.

A   *In what ways can this picture be thought to reflect ressurection?*

Study tip

In many ways the simplest example of the idea of life after death is the caterpillar–butterfly, but you have to accept that a butterfly then lives forever.

Heaven and hell

What is heaven?

The early idea of **heaven** was a place above the earth where God
dwelt. Now the idea of 'above' is seen as symbolic not literal. It is
a higher place, a state of great perfection, the bliss of being in the
presence of God. Because of these qualities, heaven is seen as a state of
reward and fulfilment, a place of great happiness.

What is hell?

The opposite of heaven is hell, a place of eternal despair and
separation from God. Hell is chosen by those who reject what God has
to offer. This rejection might be shown by the way the individual leads
his or her life on earth. To convey some idea of the pain and despair
experienced in a hell without God, believers use the images of fire
and torments. These are simply human images designed to convey
some understanding of what it means to reject God and they cannot
be taken literally. Hell is shown as a place where Satan or Iblis rules.
Satan is regarded as a fallen angel who wanted to be equal to God, the
personification of evil, who tries to get humans to reject God.

Paradise

While the term '**paradise**' can be used equally by Jews and Christians,
it is the Muslims who use the term most. For them it is the equivalent
of heaven. It is looking back to the perfection of the Garden of Eden. It
is given as a reward to those who are faithful to Allah. After the Day of
Judgement, those on the right will be taken to paradise, an ideal state
in the presence of God.

A One person's image of heaven or
paradise

Beliefs and teachings

The following passages from the Qur'an give a good idea of the Muslim view of paradise:

Not so the worshippers who are steadfast in prayer; who set aside a due portion of their goods for the needy and the dispossessed; who truly believe in the Day of Reckoning and dread the punishment of their Lord (for none is secure from the punishment of their Lord); who restrain their carnal desire ... who keep their trusts and promises and bear true witness; who attend to their prayers with promptitude. These shall be laden with honours and shall dwell in fair gardens.

Surah 70:38

When the earth shakes and quivers and the mountains crumble away and scatter abroad into fine dust, you shall be divided into three multitudes: those on the right (blessed shall be those on the right); those on the left (damned shall be those on the left); and those to the fore (foremost shall be those!). Such as they that shall be brought near to their Lord in the gardens of delight.

Surah 56:2

The Day of Judgement is the appointed time for all. On that day no man shall help his friend; none shall be helped save those on whom Allah will have mercy. He is the mighty one, the Merciful.

Surah 43:31

But the true servants of Allah shall be provided for, feasting on fruit, and honoured in the gardens of delight. Reclining face to face on soft couches, they shall be served with a goblet filled at a gushing fountain, white, and delicious to those who drink it. It will neither dull their senses nor befuddle them. They shall sit with bashful, dark-eyed virgins, as chaste as the sheltered eggs of ostriches.

Surah 37:40–37:57

▨ The validity of these beliefs

The following points could be made about these beliefs:

- No one (with the exception of Jesus, in Christian belief) has come back from the dead to tell us what life in the afterlife is like, so writers are imagining what life with or without God would be like.
- The picture-language used about heaven, hell, paradise, judgement, etc. is too physical and cannot give us any idea of what the reality is like.
- These beliefs have made sense to millions of people down the ages so they must at least reflect something that has value for people.
- Humans sense that there is more to the individual than this life would fulfil. An afterlife such as heaven completes the picture.
- The idea of punishment in hell would support the idea of God as a just God in punishing those who have done wrong and have appeared to get away with it.

Extension activity

Select other passages from Jewish, Christian or Islamic texts that reflect the ideas of Heaven, Hell and Paradise. What further information can you discover about these beliefs?

Summary

You should now understand the beliefs that heaven is a state of total happiness in the presence of God, the reward for those who have done good things in life and who welcome the presence of God; hell is the place of punishment for those who have done evil and who have rejected God; paradise is a place of reward for Muslims who are faithful to Allah.

Activities

4   Draw a picture to reflect the teaching of Islam about paradise.

5   'The images used to describe paradise are too physical to be true of the afterlife.' Do you agree? Give reasons for your answer, showing that you have thought about more than one point of view.

6   Go through each of the statements on the left and say whether you agree with it or not, explaining your answer.

7   'The teachings about eternal life make sense.' Do you agree? Give reasons for your answer, showing that you have thought about more than one point of view.

Reincarnation and rebirth

Many people find the idea of an eternal life hard to grasp, but they feel that a person has a soul or that there is an aspect of the individual that lasts beyond death. One way that these two beliefs can be combined is by the concept of either **reincarnation** or **rebirth**. These two ideas are not the same.

Reincarnation

What is reincarnation?

Reincarnation is the view held by most Hindus that when a person dies they may have another life on earth as a person or an animal. Hindus believe that a person has an immortal atman, or soul. The atman works in and through a person's body.

Escaping the cycle of reincarnation

The atman seeks to get back to Brahman (the world soul) by escaping the cycle of reincarnation. However, the soul is also attracted by the pleasures of this world that can only be enjoyed through a body, so when a body dies, the atman is drawn back to a new flesh, a new body. When the atman realises that it cannot be satisfied with what the world has to offer, the atman will seek the higher forms of happiness that can only be reached outside the body. At this point the atman reaches moksha, or liberation; it has escaped the cycle of reincarnation.

Reincarnation and karma

Many Hindus believe that the quality of life a person experiences in this life now is affected by their karma. Karma is the law of consequences in which good actions build up good karma and bad actions build up bad karma. If a person leads an ultimately good life, free from too many negative attachments to this world, the next reincarnation will be of a higher order of existence. For many Hindus some forms of life are better (higher) or worse (lower) than others. When people are reincarnated they either go up to a better form of life or down to a worse one.

Reincarnation is fair	Reincarnation is not fair
Because of the connection with karma, many people think that there is great justice shown in the Hindu reincarnation cycle. The good are rewarded and the bad punished, and everyone has as much time as is needed to escape reincarnation and achieve liberation when the soul joins Brahman.	Some people feel that this system shows great injustice: if a person is a combination of a soul and a body, why should this particular combination of soul and body be punished (or rewarded) for something that was done by the atman in a different body?

A *Is reincarnation fair?*

For Sikhs, a person's soul is reborn into another body when they die, and this might be either another human being or an animal. The state

Objectives

Know and understand what is meant by reincarnation and rebirth.

Understand what these teachings show about the nature and value of life.

Evaluate the validity of these beliefs.

Key terms

Rebirth: in Buddhism, the belief that after this life there is continuity into a new life form that is affected by the karma gained so far.

Reincarnation: the Hindu belief that after this life the soul moves on to a new, usually bodily, form.

∞ links

For more on karma, rebirth and reincarnation see page 96.

Extension activity

1 Use the internet and/or a library to investigate the idea of the Hindu caste system and how it reflects certain Hindu ideas about reincarnation.

of the next life depends on how well the person led their former life. However, it is only through the human body that a person can find the Oneness with God that brings to an end the cycle of reincarnation.

Remembering previous reincarnations

Some people claim that there is evidence that people can remember who they were or what happened to them in the last reincarnation. Given the millions of people who are believed to have been reincarnated, the percentage of people who can remember anything at all is very small. Some people would dismiss the odd example of people remembering things as just a strange experience, not as a real remembrance.

Rebirth

Rebirth is the belief usually held by Buddhists. They do not believe that there is an atman or soul that moves from one body to another. However, there is a sense of continuity between the different people. A simple image is lighting one candle from another there is some connection between the new light and the old one, but they are not the same.

Escaping the cycle of rebirth

Rebirth is connected with samsara, the wheel of suffering. The Four Noble Truths (all is suffering, suffering comes from craving, to end suffering you must get rid of craving, the way to get rid of craving is to follow the Noble Eight fold Path) help a person to escape the cycle of rebirth by reaching nibbana. People can be helped by the example of a Bodhisattva. A Bodhisattva is an enlightened being who stays in the cycle of rebirth to enable others to attain enlightenment.

Rebirth and karma

For many Buddhists there are six realms of rebirth: three are pleasant (peaceful gods, power-seeking gods and humans) and three are unpleasant (animals, hungry ghosts and hell-beings). The type of realm a person enters on rebirth is determined by their karma (the actions of body, speech and mind).

B   *For Buddhists a Bodhisattva gives an example to help others attain enlightenment*

Summary

You should now know and understand what is meant by reincarnation and rebirth. Most Hindus and Sikhs believe in reincarnation; that the atman (soul) comes back in another body until it attains liberation. The karma acquired in one life will decide the quality of the reincarnated life. Most Buddhists believe in rebirth. Buddhists believe that to escape from the cycle of rebirth a person needs to accept the four noble truths and follow the eight fold path.

Out-of-body and near-death experiences

During the 20th century, there has been an increase in the number of people who claim that they have had out-of-body and near-death experiences. The reason for this increase could simply be that medical treatment is now so good that people can be helped to recover from injuries or operations which, in the past, would have killed them. People have questioned whether these experiences prove anything about what exists after death.

Out-of-body experiences

In many cultures there have been wise men or shamans who, people believed, could make contact with the spirit or go out of their body and experience events elsewhere. There are now quite frequent reports of 'normal' people also experiencing out-of-body experiences. This is more than dreaming, though some of the experiences are said to have taken place when the person's body was asleep.

Arguments about out-of-body experiences

Many reported cases like the one in the case study, each one fairly simple, do raise questions about whether the soul can survive outside the body. If it can, then it raises questions about what happens to the soul at death, when the body ceases to function. The logical answer might be that the soul continues elsewhere, but there is no way of proving this.

Some people claim that their spirit or soul is totally separable from their body. In many cultures, there is the belief that the soul can leave the body. Some people who have taken drugs say that they have felt their soul leave their bodies, but is this simply a delusion caused by the effect of the drug? Some people think that a person who uses a drug has created an out-of-body experience. However, does this prove that it is only the drug that has caused the experience or could it simply be that the drug has opened up that person to receiving the experience?

There are cases of people who doubted that out-of-body experiences were possible and yet have reported later that they have had such an experience. This might suggest that there is an outside cause for out–of-body experiences.

Near-death experiences

There are some common elements in **near-death experiences** that have led some people to question whether they actually prove there is life after death.

Raymond Moody, in America in the 1970s, drew up a list of typical factors from accounts of near-death experiences he had come across. These include:

- the person hears themselves pronounced dead
- the presence of a loud buzzing or ringing noise and a long, dark tunnel

Objectives

Know and understand what is meant by out-of-body and near-death experiences.

Understand what some people claim that these experiences show about an afterlife.

Evaluate the importance of these ideas.

Case study

An out-of-body experience

Some people claim that they have felt themselves looking down at their own body from a distance. There have been accounts of people undergoing surgery who have seen the operation from above. One doctor, when he was being operated on, claimed he went into the neighbouring operating theatre where a young child was in great distress. He noticed that the child had a broken rib that had been overlooked by those caring for the child. When the doctor awoke, he reported the child's condition and he was proved to be correct.

Activities

1. Find at least one account of an out-of-body experience (the internet has quite a number on different sites). How truthful do you think this account is? Explain your answer.

2. 'Out of body experiences are just the imagination running wild.' What do you think? Explain your opinion.

Key terms

Near-death experience: some people, when they are close to death, claim to have had a sense of themselves leaving their bodies and seeing what exists beyond this life.

- the person sees their own body from a distance and watches what is happening
- the person meets others and a 'being of light' who shows them a playback of events from their life and helps them to evaluate it
- the person reaches a barrier and knows that they has to go back
- even though they feel joy, love and peace there, the person returns to their body and life.

A   *Are out-of-body experiences for real?*

Case study

A near-death experience

In 1991, Pam Reynolds underwent a brain operation. She was put under anaesthesia and her eyes taped shut. During part of the operation, Pam's heart stopped beating, she had no brain wave activity and no blood flowing to her brain, meaning that she was clinically dead.

Pam felt a strange sensation – she 'popped' out of her body and floated up in the air. From her position above the operating table, she observed her motionless body being operated on. Later, Pam was able to tell nurses in great detail about things that had been said and done during the operation.

Eventually, Pam moved away from the operating room and found herself being pulled down a 'tunnel' towards a bright light. In the light, Pam recognised people who were waiting for her, including her grandmother who had died a long time before.

Soon, a man she recognised as her dead uncle took her back to the operating room. Pam re-entered her body, which she said felt like diving into a pool of ice water.

Discussion activity

As a class, debate the topic: 'Science can explain near death experiences.'

Arguments about near-death experiences

There are some scientists who question the cause of these experiences (but who accept that the people have experienced something that seemed real to them). When the brain is in a stressful situation it can produce chemicals that can create extreme sensations. Perhaps these chemicals stimulate the brain to produce this type of picture imagery.

No matter how many people claim to have this type of experience, there will never be any definitive proof that these experiences show that there is anything beyond this life. One interesting aspect of these accounts, however, is that the experiences are often very similar, regardless of the society or religion the people belonged to. This suggests that the people are not simply repeating something that they have learned or picked up as they were growing up.

Activity

3   'Near-death experiences prove that there is life after death.' Do you agree? Give reasons for your answer, showing that you have thought about more than one point of view.

Summary

You should now know and understand what is meant by out-of-body and near-death experiences, and that they raise questions about what happens to the soul at death. These experiences do not prove that there is a life after death, but some people believe that these experiences suggest that there could be life after death.

How belief in the afterlife affects this life: Judaism, Christianity and Islam

In all the major religions there is a direct relationship between what a person does and is in this life and what happens in the afterlife. In some cases what happens after death is directly connected with the deeds a person performs. In other cases it has more to do with what a person believes, but even here the belief expresses itself through actions. This means that believers need to be aware of their actions and that they might do the right action specifically for a reward in the afterlife. For some people this might raise questions about the acceptability of particular actions, especially if there is no element of a person performing a deed simply to help another human being in need.

THE END OF THE WORLD IS NIGH!

A *How would people react if they took this warning seriously?*

Judaism

In the later books of the Jewish scriptures, there is teaching about God's judgement of the whole world. Particularly in the books of the prophets, there are promises about the Day of the Lord. This day is seen as the moment when either the Messiah will come in his power or God's judgement will be passed on the whole world. After that day, the chosen people will live in the perfect state.

What these passages deal with are the types of attitudes and lifestyle that God expects from his people. In the beliefs and teachings passage it promises that the people will live as God wants and they will not be afraid because God is looking after them. It is a return to the Garden of Eden situation before the Fall of Adam and Eve. While the focus of these passages is in the future, the challenge for the Jews is to try to live this way now. In this way, at the end, everyone will live out the relationship with God. The future should just be an extension of the present.

Beliefs and teachings

'The remnant of Israel will do no wrong; they will speak no lies, nor will deceit be found in their mouths. They will eat and lie down and no one will make them afraid.'

Zephaniah 3:13

Christianity

In Christianity, judgement and reward are clearly linked together in many of the teachings. The teaching is made very clear in the Parable of the Last Judgement (Matthew 25: 31–46).

Christians are challenged to do good works now, not just because they want to be rewarded, but because there are people in need and it is their duty to help, regardless of rewards. They are to treat others as they would treat Jesus. The motives for good action might not be the hope of 'reward'. However, the message of Christianity is quite clear: there is a direct connection between actions in this world and what happens to a person in the afterlife.

Islam

Similarly in Islam, the Day of Judgement will be the day on which those who are faithful to Allah will be rewarded and those who reject Allah will be punished.

Beliefs and teachings

7And call in remembrance the favour of Allah unto you, and His covenant, which He ratified with you, when ye said: 'We hear and we obey': And fear Allah, for Allah knoweth well the secrets of your hearts.

8O ye who believe! stand out firmly for Allah, as witnesses to fair dealing, and let not the hatred of others to you make you swerve to wrong and depart from justice. Be just: that is next to piety: and fear Allah. For Allah is well-acquainted with all that ye do.

9To those who believe and do deeds of righteousness hath Allah promised forgiveness and a great reward.

10Those who reject faith and deny our signs will be companions of Hell-fire.

Qur'an, Surah 5

As with Christianity and Judaism, the rewards in Islam are for specific actions and attitudes and will apply equally to all people. The challenge for believers in these three religions is to continually live their lives with a view to the end of time. The goal is to be with God forever. Since these people believe they only have one life to live through before final judgement, it is important that believers live their lives to the full and follow the teachings of their religion.

Summary

You should now understand that many religions focus on the deeds performed in this life. Many believe that, in the afterlife, good deeds will be rewarded and bad deeds punished. The attitude when performing a deed is also important for religions. Many people do good deeds because they feel these actions are pleasing to God.

 links

Read the Parable of the Last Judgement (Matthew 25: 31–46) and use it to inform your answer in activity 1 if you choose Christianity.

Research activity

2   Choose one of these three religions. Research and present its teachings about judgement and the afterlife.

Extension activity

Examine five passages from Judaism, Christianity and Islam that deal with the idea of judgement. Compare the beliefs of these religions.

Discussion activity

Draw up the arguments you would use in a debate on the topic: 'People only live good lives to ensure a better afterlife.'

Activity

'Believers have an advantage because they want to be good all the time and so find good actions easier to perform.' Do you agree? Give reasons for your answer, showing that you have thought about more than one point of view.

How belief in the afterlife affects this life: Eastern religions

Those religions that believe in reincarnation equally stress the need to live good lives this time round. Karma is built up and will decide what happens in the next cycle, so a believer cannot afford to live badly.

Buddhism

In Buddhism the challenge is to get beyond the cravings, to reach nibbana. To do this a Buddhist has to try to live a perfect life, living by the four noble truths and the eight fold path. Everything Buddhists do must help them escape from the cycle of rebirth. The focus of action and attitude must be to accept that all this world has to offer can be misleading. A proper attitude towards this life can help a Buddhist to see through these limitations.

Beliefs and teachings

That which is of bitter taste is bound to be good medicine.
That which sounds unpleasant to the ear is certainly frank advice.
By amending our mistakes, we get wisdom.
By defending our faults, we betray an unsound mind.
In our daily life we should always practise altruism, But Buddhahood is not to be attained by giving away money as charity.
Bodhi is to be found within our own mind,

Note: Bodhi is the enlightenment that enables a person to see through the delusions of this life. Altruism is the ability to put other people's needs before your own; to do what is good for them no matter the cost to yourself.

The Sutra of the 6th Patriarch, Hui Neng. **Bhagavad Gita** *Chapter 3 verse 19, 31*

Hinduism

Beliefs and teachings

Therefore, without being attached to the fruits of activities, one should act as a matter of duty, for by working without attachment one attains the Supreme.

Bhagavad Gita 3.19

Those persons who execute their duties according to My injunctions and who follow this teaching faithfully, without envy, become free from the bondage of actions that have consequences.

Bhagavad Gita 3.31

A good Hindu will do the right action regardless of his personal feelings about what he has to do. The action will be right. This comes out clearly in the conversation between Arjuana, a warrior prince who does not feel it is right to fight and kill his cousins, and Krishna, who tells him to do his duty without passion.

The Sutra of the 6th Patriarch, Hui Neng. **Bhagavad Gita** *Chapter 3 verse 19, 31*

Objectives

Understand that people might be influenced in the way they live in this life by their hope for the afterlife.

Know and understand how these beliefs affect the way people live.

Evaluate whether people only live good lives to ensure a better afterlife.

These passages guide Hindus to do all actions without thinking about their personal gain. If people want specific things to come from their actions, even if the outcomes are very good and worthwhile, it means that they are still too attached to this life to escape reincarnation. Good Hindus do what is required without thinking of their own feelings or the results.

Sikhism

Sikhs aim to find union with God and escape from reincarnation. The only way they can do this is by becoming free from attachments and worldly thoughts. They are called to live by the truth, to meditate upon God and to give charity to those in need. This will be reinforced by hard work and looking for justice for all people in all aspects of life. This positive attitude to life and its demands will help the Sikh to come closer to God in this life and to escape the cycle of reincarnation.

A   *Meditation can help Sikhs to free their minds from worldly attachments*

Activities

1   Do you think it is possible to do actions without being affected by them? Explain your answer.

2   'People only do the right actions to be rewarded.' Do you agree? Give reasons for your answer, showing that you have thought about more than one point of view.

Research activity

Use the internet and/or a library to investigate the life style of a Buddhist monk. How does this lifestyle reflect their beliefs about the afterlife?

Extension activity

Examine five passages from Buddhist, Hindu and Sikh sacred texts. What teachings can you find about how to live in this life in order to achieve a better afterlife? Examine the differences between these religions on these topics.

Discussion activity

As a class, debate the topic: "Beliefs about reincarnation have a greater impact on the life of the believer than beliefs about resurrection and judgement."

Summary

You should now understand that many religions focus on the deeds performed in this life. They believe that good deeds will be rewarded and bad deeds punished.

Study tip

You are not required to know what each individual religion teaches on these issues, but you do need to be aware of the general approaches to these topics that religions take.

6

The afterlife – summary

For the examination you should now be able to:

✓ know and understand evidence for and against the existence of an afterlife

✓ understand the ideas of eternal life, heaven, paradise, resurrection, reincarnation and rebirth and the arguments for and against these beliefs

✓ understand and evaluate accounts of out of body and near death experiences

✓ know and understand how the different beliefs in the afterlife affect the way believers live in this life.

Sample answer

1 Write an answer to the following exam question:

How valid are out-of-body and near-death experiences as proof of continued existence after death?   *(6 marks)*

2 Read the following sample answer.

> People claim that they have had out of body experiences when they were in operating rooms. These accounts often talk about hearing conversations that have actually taken place, even though the patient was unconscious. Near-death experiences often talk of going towards a bright light. But all we have are accounts of people in very extreme situations and we don't know how their bodies are reacting to the medications etc., so why should we pay any attention to what they have to say?

3 With a partner, discuss the sample answer. Do you think there are other things the student could have included in the answer?

4 What mark would you give this answer out of 6? Look at the mark scheme in the Introduction on page 7 (AO1). What are the reasons for the mark you have given?

Practice questions

1   Read the extract below and answer the following questions.

> 66 *Multitudes who sleep in the dust of the earth will awake: some to everlasting life, others to shame and everlasting contempt.* 99
>
> *Daniel 12:2*

(a) Explain what types of beliefs about life after death are shown in this passage.   *(3 marks)*

> **Study tip** Remember in (a) to study the stimulus material carefully and use information from it in your answer.

(b) Explain two pieces of evidence that people might put forward to justify belief in life after death.   *(4 marks)*

> **Study tip** Remember in (b) that you have to give two pieces of evidence. There will be two marks available for each piece and you will lose marks if you only give one piece of evidence.

(c) 'Believers' lives are not affected by what they believe about life after death.' What do you think? Explain your answer.   *(3 marks)*

(d) 'Rebirth and reincarnation make sense of life after death.' What do you think? Explain your answer.   *(3 marks)*

> **Study tip** Remember that these are only 3-mark evaluation questions so you only have to present one side of the argument. However, it is important to justify your opinion.

Glossary

A

99 Beautiful Names of Allah: the tiles used by Muslims to proclaim the qualities of Allah.

Adam and Eve: the first man and woman in the Judaeo-Christian tradition who committed the first sin.

Agnostic: a person who does not know if there is a God or not.

All-compassionate God: cares for the weaknesses of people and is concerned about them.

All-knowing God: knows everything that there is to be known.

All-loving God: creates all things in his loving and caring nature so there is nothing outside concern.

All-merciful God: is willing to forgive people but in a way that accepts the need for justice

All-powerful God: can do anything that can be done; there is nothing outside God's ability.

Argument from design: a proof for the existence of God based on the idea that there is so much design and purpose in the universe that it could not have happened by accident; there has to have been a designer, God. Otherwise called the teleological argument.

Atheist: a person who believes that there is no God.

B

Benevolent: another word for all-loving showing that God wants what is best for his creatures.

Big bang: many scientists think that the universe began with an explosion from which everything that makes up the universe came into being.

C

Characteristics: features or qualities that are typical of that being.

Compassionate: one of the qualities of God, showing concern for the sufferings of others; literally 'suffering with'.

Compatibility: when two or more different ideas can be used together without problems or tension.

Congruent: when two or more ideas come together in harmony.

Cosmological: to do with the nature of the universe. Used in particular with the cosmological argument that says there has to be a God to explain the existence of all things.

Creation: everything in the Universe, especially when seen as a specific work of God.

D

Daddy: an intimate name used to address your father.

Darwinian view: named after Charles Darwin who pioneered the idea of evolution; the idea that creatures have gradually changed and adapted to suit the environment, "the survival of the fittest."

Designer: the one who arranges for the various parts of an object to come together so that the object can fulfil its purpose.

Dreams: series of images that occur in the mind during sleep.

E

Enlightenment: the gaining of true knowledge, particularly in the Buddhist tradition, that frees a person from the cycle of rebirth by seeing what the truth about life really is.

Eternal: without limits in time; outside time.

Evidence: information that proves whether an idea or fact is valid.

Evil: the opposite of good. A force or a negative power that is seen in many traditions as destructive and against God.

Evolution: the process made popular by Charles Darwin that describes how simpler life-forms gradually changed and adapted to more complex life forms.

Existence: that which has objective reality; that which truly is.

Experience: the awareness that is gained from an event particularly by using the senses and emotions.

F

Faith: a commitment to something that goes beyond proof and knowledge, especially used about God and religion.

Father: a man in relation to his children; the one who cares and provides for his offspring.

Feminine: the words that usually refer to the female.

First cause argument: otherwise known as the cosmological argument. A proof for the existence of God based on the idea that there had to be an uncaused cause that made everything else happen otherwise there would be nothing now.

Five ways: the five different but related proofs that Thomas Aquinas produced to show that there must be a God.

Forms: the different ways in which people picture God.

Forgiveness: letting someone off when they have hurt or offended you. To give someone another chance.

Free will: the ability of human beings to make their own choices.

Free will defence: an argument to justify both the existence of a loving God and the existence of evil. It is based on the idea that what makes humans special is their ability to choose. For this to happen they have to live in a world in which things can, and do, go wrong.

Fundamentalist: a person who believes in the basics of a religion, particularly believing that what is contained in the sacred text is an accurate, almost factual, record that cannot be questioned.

G

General revelation: the belief that God can be known by anybody who is prepared to accept the idea that through creation e.g. nature, God shows his true nature.

God: the supreme being who has no limits in time, space or power

Godhead: the divine nature, all the qualities that belong to God.

H

Harmony: things working together to produce a pleasing effect.

He: the word that is used to refer to man, boy or male animal but which is usually also used when there is not a specific mention of the sex of the person being referred to.

Heaven: the state of eternal happiness in the presence of God that Christians believe will be granted to the faithful after this life.

Hell: the place of suffering in the afterlife without the presence of God for those who are damned.

I

Iblis: the angel who rejected Allah's wishes and fell from Paradise in the Islamic tradition.

Idolatry: treating a limited object as a God and offering the object worship.

Illusion: a false idea or belief often based on a wrong impression

Immanent: the idea that God is very close and is involved in what goes on in the world. He is not distant or uncaring

Imperfection: a fault or limitation or lack of completeness. This shows that the thing described is not as good as it could or should be.

Impersonal: the idea that God is a force or abstract idea, and cannot be described in human terms

Infinity: that which has no limits in space or time.

Intelligent design: a response by fundamentalists to the idea of evolution. While there might be some acceptance of variations within species as suggested by evolution, this theory says that all these variations are the work of God.

Intention: the purpose underlying an action that gives the action meaning.

J

Judgement: the belief that after death people will be assessed on the amount of good and bad things that they have done and will be rewarded or punished accordingly.

K

Karma: a belief in Hinduism and Buddhism that a person's good and bad actions in this life and in previous lives contribute to the quality of future lives.

King: the male ruler who governs a country.

L

Liberal: a person who believes that the sacred text has truths in it but that these truths need to be interpreted in the text.

Love: to have a deep affection for and a great interest in another.

M

Masculine: the words that usually refer to the male.

Merciful: a quality of God that stresses God's willingness to forgive the wrongdoer.

Monotheist: a person who believes that there is only one God

Moral evil: the harm that results from a bad choice made by human beings misusing their free will.

N

Near death experience: some people, when they are close to death, claim to have had a sense of themselves leaving their bodies and seeing what exists beyond this life.

Natural evil: the harm or damage that is done to people and creation as a result of the forces of nature and the structure of the Earth.

Nature of God: the qualities that combine to make up what God is.

O

Omnipotent: another word for 'all-powerful'.

Omniscient: another word meaning 'all-knowing'.

Oneness: the idea of being a complete whole that cannot be divided in any way.

Order: the arrangement of the parts of an object or event that shows there is a particular purpose behind this object or event.

Origin: where something begins.

Out of body experiences: the feeling that the person is freed from the limitations of the body for a time.

P

Paradise: the ideal place in which the faithful are rewarded for all eternity; a name used about heaven especially by Muslims.

Personal: when used about God, the idea that God cares about the individual and is involved in the individual's life.

Philosophy: literally 'the love of wisdom'. The study of ideas and the nature of knowledge and existence.

Pictures: images or drawings that try to represent a reality or an idea.

Prayer: talking to God especially as praise or a solemn request for help.Proof: the evidence that establishes a fact

Pure being: something that exists in its own right and does not depend on anything else. Pure Being cannot be broken down into smaller parts.

R

Reality: things as they truly are.

Rebirth: in Buddhism, the belief that after this life there is a continuity into a new life form that is affected by the karma gained so far.

Reincarnation: the Hindu belief that after this life the soul moves on to a new, usually bodily, form.

Relational: the way two or more beings interact and respond to each other.

Religion: a unified system of beliefs and practice that often relates to an outside force or God.

Resurrection: the Christian belief that Jesus rose from the dead and entered into eternal life and that all souls will join in this resurrection on the Last Day.

Revelation: God shows himself to believers; this is the only way anybody can really know anything about God.

Reward: the idea of getting back something good in return for what you have done right.

S

Sacred texts: books and documents that believers accept as having a special connection with God or their religious beliefs.

Satan: another name for the Devil, the fallen angel.

Soul: the spiritual or immaterial part of the person that is seen as being eternal.

Soul-making: the belief that suffering makes it possible for people to 'grow' into more mature individuals.

Special revelation: God shows himself to an individual or group of individuals in a specific, direct way, as opposed to general revelation.

Steady state theory: the belief that the universe is a constant feature and that there is a constant move from energy to matter within the universe.

Suffering: the experience of something bad or painful.

T

Teleological: to do with design or order, particularly the attempt to prove the existence of God by showing that there is design and order in the universe.

Theist: a person who believes that there is a God who is directly involved in creation.

The Truth: the Sikh name for God showing that God is perfect and without any deceptions.

Transcendent: the belief that God is beyond space and time, and that there are no limitations on what he can do

Trimurti: the three central gods or aspects of God in Hinduism: Brahma, Vishnu and Shiva

Trinity: the Christian belief that in the One God there are Three Persons, God the Father, God the Son and God the Holy Spirit.

Trust: the ability to accept that the person or being will look after your needs.

U

Ultimate questions: those matters that cannot easily be addressed but which affect the way most people respond to life, e.g. is there a God? What happens after death? Etc.

Universe: all that exists in matter and space seen as a single thing.

V

Valid: something that supports the truth of a statement or fact.

Vision: seeing something, especially in a dream or trance, that shows something about the nature of God or the afterlife.

W

Words: parts of speech that are used to convey meaning.

Index